The Road God Walks

The Road God Walks

by

Germaine Copeland

Harrison House
Tulsa, Oklahoma

The Road God Walks
ISBN 1-57794-299-X
Copyright © 2000 by Germaine Copeland
38 Sloan Street
Roswell, Georgia 30075

Published by Harrison House, Inc.
P. O. Box 35035
Tulsa, Oklahoma 74153

Dedication

To Everette, my husband

And our children,

David, Renee, Terri and Lynn

Contents

Acknowledgments 9

Preface 11

Introduction 13

CHAPTER 1 A Time To Pray...15

CHAPTER 2 Personal Growth Through Prayer 23

CHAPTER 3 What Is Prayer? 49

CHAPTER 4 Pray in Agreement With God's Will 71

CHAPTER 5 Purposes of Intercessory Prayer 95

CHAPTER 6 Wisdom in Prayer...107

CHAPTER 7 Who Is Called To Pray? 131

CHAPTER 8 Preparing for Intercession 147

CHAPTER 9 Praying for a Loved One 165

CHAPTER 10 What Is Spiritual Warfare? 173

CHAPTER 11 Prayer Group Guidelines.....................................195

Acknowledgments

While this book is about my personal spiritual development and emotional healing, I am indebted to those who have encouraged and inspired me. I thank my neighbors and fellow believers who attended the first Bible studies in which I did my "student teaching." I would like to thank those who united with me in prayer throughout the years: Doris Beasley, my first prayer partner; Lois Carole Price, the first prayer director for Word Ministries and those who followed. They were patient with me, and we learned, grew and achieved levels of prayer that availed much. Also, Andrell Stevens, editor; the Harrison House team; my present staff and my prayer partners deserve my applause and appreciation. Words do not adequately express the gratitude that is in my heart. Please accept my heartfelt thank you for your love and support.

"**M**y life is the road God walks."

I do not remember where I first read these words. It seemed that suddenly, they were emblazoned on the portals of my mind and on my heart. They would not let me go. As I wrote and rewrote this book, I recognized what I'd learned long ago: that the narrative of each life is portrayed on God's eternal landscape and we are all interconnected.

Each life is like an eternal highway, never ending, but always leading either to a brighter day or on into the darkness. As I observed this canvas, I recognized unlit roads with many obstacles waiting for the light. Other pathways were rocky with detours. Here and there was a glimmer of light, and as I continued to look, there appeared roads that emanated radiant beams of glorious light. All along each roadway were signposts pointing to life eternal.

This life of mine appeared, and I recognized the familiar, dark, dead-end street. I was a non-entity. The "arteries" that exited my road led to more frustration, and I discovered that there was no way out. Where could I go, except backwards? I couldn't undo years of wrong decisions. It seemed that there was no going back.

How could I get past the end of the road? Occasionally, I would tunnel through a dead end, only to run into another dead end—a road leading nowhere. Where could I go? I couldn't get past the obstacles. I couldn't get over them. Where was God? Where was love?

That was my life—I was trapped, restless and yearning, yet I always knew that somewhere was joy and peace.

But on the most memorable day of my life, light finally broke through, and the road—my life—was lit with a brilliancy that exceeds description. And not only were my eyes flooded with light, but I was also absorbed by *the* Light—my entire being *became* light.

This book is about my personal spiritual journey. God lives in me. He has made His home in me. Where I go, He goes. And my life is the road God walks.

The *Prayers That Avail Much Family Series* are the prayers I wrote as I faced obstacles and victories on the pathway of life. Many voices call out, but I follow the Light that becomes brighter and brighter. The road God walks is filled with righteousness, peace, love and joy. Jesus is the Lord, the Master of my life.

Along with my experiences I have included teachings that the Holy Spirit revealed to my heart. The motivating force of my life is to experience God, to know Him intimately as we walk together. He dwells in me, and I abide in Him. Our lives are intertwined.

—Germaine Copeland

"**H**ere we are."

The car stopped on a quiet, residential street in Phoenix, Arizona. Taking a deep breath, I reached for my briefcase, opened the car door and walked with my friend, Susan, to the house where I would be speaking to a large Bible study and prayer group. Our hostess led us into her spacious, beautifully decorated home. She guided us to the buffet, pausing occasionally to introduce me to smiling people who seemed to be everywhere.

Balancing my plate, napkin, flatware and beverage while threading my way through the crowd, I found a place to sit. Out of the corner of my eye, I saw someone advancing toward me. I quickly prepared to acknowledge another introduction. I looked up and saw a tall, attractive woman clutching a gray leather book—*Prayers That Avail Much, Special Edition.* Without introductions, she held up the book and declared, "This book changed my life! I have given away at least one hundred copies."

"That book changed my life, too!" I exclaimed.

Looking disappointed, she said, "Oh, but I thought you were the author."

Smiling, I answered, "I am. The prayers in that book are the prayers that changed my life. Now I have the privilege of sharing them with others."

But before I ever wrote those prayers from my heart, I had an experience with God that turned my life around forever. God supernaturally took me off my own path of depression and despair and showed me the road that He walks. That incredible journey—learning to walk the road God walks—is exactly what I want to share with you.

CHAPTER 1

A Time To Pray

M y present surroundings dim as calendar years quickly roll back, and I remember the events of a day in January 1968 when God's presence permeated my kitchen. I vividly recall the events and emotion of that day, even though it was more than thirty years ago.

Our three older children were in school, and after placing the baby in her crib for a nap, I returned to the kitchen to eat lunch in solitude. Outside the skies were overcast; the bleakness of the day matched my mood. I continued to linger over my cup of coffee, sitting motionless as many scenes played in my head. Thoughts I wouldn't dare share with others bombarded and tormented me: *Look at you. It's afternoon, and your work isn't done. Your mother was right. You are lazy!*

As the accusations mounted, so did my feelings of condemnation and self-pity. *Other women work outside the home and get their housework done,* I thought. *Look at all the unfinished projects you've started. You never complete anything! Why don't you just leave? Everette is a much better parent than you are. Your children would be much better off without you.*

The inner turmoil began. *Leave my husband and children?* I thought. *Where can I go? What can I do?*

When Everette and I married, I had expected to live happily ever after. With the birth of each child, I anticipated that I would find the contentment that eluded me. But I did not.

What's wrong with me, God? I prayed. *Is this all there is to life? Why did You make me so different? You really made a mistake when I was born. If only I had been the one to die young and my baby sister had lived instead. Not only is my life chaotic, but I'm hurting my husband and children. They really would be better off without me.*

Failure and Depression:
A Never-Ending Cycle

A quick review of my life reassured me that I was indeed thinking rationally. In my early teens, I had discovered the world of fiction novels. I became addicted to the flights into fantasy they offered. But now reading the classics or the latest bestseller no longer soothed my shame and heartache.

After marriage and the birth of our first child, the real demands of daily life forced me to emerge from my world of fiction. I eased into my new reality by reading books on marriage and parenting. One by one, the books offered advice and instructions that seemed to prove I didn't measure up.

Again I felt like a failure. No matter how many books I read or how hard I tried to be a good wife and mother, I was a flop. I felt crushed beneath boulders of guilt. My furtive attempts at perfection resulted in utter futility. It was impossible, so why try any longer? I couldn't please anyone, not even myself.

Every other month, I pondered a new possibility in my search for a sense of accomplishment. *If only I had a piano*, I thought, *I could continue the study of classical music.* Surely that was a goal I could easily attain to provide the fulfillment I craved.

I promised Everette I would teach piano in order to pay for such an expensive purchase. But after a few months, I could no longer face the students, and Everette still had to make the payments. Another failure. Gradually I slowed to an eventual stop in my own studies.

Even preparing to teach the three-year-olds in Sunday school had overwhelmed me—so much so that I quit attending church. Besides, getting my own four children dressed and out the door was more than I could handle.

How many of my enthusiastic attempts to find my niche had resulted only in failure! All I wanted was to succeed at *something*. All I seemed to do was fail at *everything*.

Momentarily, I considered the sleeping pills in my medicine cabinet. The thought of consuming them, never to awake, appeared to be the perfect solution for everyone.

Shutting out my surroundings, I plunged into a surreal state of despair. Out of the darkness a contemptuous voice assaulted my mind: *If you were really going to take those pills, you would do it now! You're kidding yourself. You don't even have the courage to take your own life. Just look at yourself. You're so weak!*

Lamely I argued, "I can't leave my baby with no one to look after her. I'll wait until Everette is home."

The voice sneered, *Ha! See what I mean? You're a failure. If you had the courage to kill yourself, you'd do it right now. Remember, even your pastor said you're a weak person.*

The voice was winning the big debate. As I yielded to thoughts of dying, I entered a place of tranquility.

Then a discomforting thought shattered my surreal peace: *What would happen if I didn't die or if someone discovered me too soon? What would my children think?*

Jolted by the thought, I realized I couldn't take my own life. But not wanting to live, I prayed a simple yet earnest prayer: "God, I've looked for someone who could erase my pain. If You are God, please help me."

God Intervenes

Suddenly a great Light came into my kitchen. Radiant beams focused on the very spot where I sat. The yellow walls seemed to vibrate with life, and everything appeared new. The world inside and outside was bathed in purity, and I sat mesmerized, wondering what was happening.

As I looked out the window, the sky seemed bluer than blue and the grass greener than green, and my mind opened to fathom knowledge beyond my awareness. Answers surfaced before I asked. Before I called, He answered.

My kitchen disappeared, and a field of hardened, brown, crusty, fallow ground stretched out across a brilliant, endless space. Gazing upon the landscape, I saw that there was more to *life* than I had ever known existed!

A passage of Scripture in *The Message Bible* illustrates the essence of that moment: **What came into existence was Life, and the Life was Light to live by** (John 1:4).

As the vision unfolded before me, I saw the Holy Spirit plowing the unbroken field. Beneath the stiff, dry ground was moist, fertile soil. A dam broke within me, and I began to sob almost violently as furrow after furrow was plowed.

As all the memories and emotion from countless hurts and disappointments rushed back to me, I heard another voice—the voice of the Holy Spirit speaking to my spirit, saying, *Old things have passed away, and behold, all things have become new.* (2 Cor. 5:17.) God was preparing the ground of my heart for the planting of His Word.

Delivered From Depression

This wondrous Person moved in and delivered me from depression—a mental disorder that I would later learn to resist and stand against. The Word of God became my medicine. He sent forth His Word and healed me, rescuing me from the pit and destruction. (Ps. 107:20.)

Depression has become an epidemic in the past few years. It is one of Satan's key tactics to defeat the body of Christ and render lives dysfunctional. Those closest to me said I was depressed because I wanted to be.

They turned away when I screamed, "I hate my behavior! I hate the way I feel, I hate life, I hate me! If only I could change and be a different person!"

No one understood that I was fighting a mental disease that's just as real as cancer is a physical disease. To tell someone caught in a battle with depression to "get over it" or "just make a decision" does not offer comfort or stimulate hope.

But God, who commanded the light to shine out of darkness, shone in my heart to give me the light of the knowledge of His glory. (2 Cor. 4:6.)

A brand-new world beckoned me. I arose from my depression to embark upon a spiritual journey that continues even to this day. I began to believe in miracles, for I had just received one. And I began to believe in God with a passion as never before. On that day, I was filled with an inexpressible and glorious joy, for I began receiving the goal of my faith: the salvation of my soul. (1 Peter 1:8,9.)

The love that flooded me that day was living proof that God had visited me. I eagerly awaited the children's arrival from school, meeting them with a smile that refused to turn into a frown. The depression and confusion left, darkness turned to day and I was changed—in a moment, in the twinkling of an eye.

The allure of escape through fantasy no longer charmed me. Instead, a hunger for reality—God's health—consumed me. As I turned my attention to God's Word, I discovered I was reading His love letter to me. I began reading my Bible voraciously. God's promises weren't general. They were personal and specific; they were exceedingly great and precious.

I stepped into a covenant relationship with a personal God who loved me unconditionally, and I was not afraid. This God was more than just an "All-Seeing Eye," peering at my every mistake. He was a loving Father. His all-seeing eye became a watchful, caring eye, looking out for my best interest and the best interests of those I love.

Thank God for His mercy and grace! The Holy Spirit became my Teacher. He revealed the things of Jesus to me—and to know Jesus is to know God, my Father.

My devotional reading turned into personal fellowship with the triune Being, and our relationship became more and more intimate. I talked with Him about everything, and He talked with me.

Sometimes as I sat with my Bible open, I would say, "Father, the Lord is my Shepherd, and I do not lack for any good or beneficial thing. I just want to fellowship with You." My contentment knew no bounds.

The Beginning of
Prayers That Avail Much

A short time later, a bombshell exploded in our home, and I asked the Holy Spirit to teach me how to pray about it. We talked with teachers, counselors, psychologists and psychiatrists, only to discover that there was no human solution to our problem. It became more vital than ever before to know how to pray prayers that avail much. Each day with my Bible, pen and notebook, I read, cried, talked with the Holy Spirit and made notes. Someone recommended a book on prayer, and I devoured its contents.

There in the inner chamber of prayer, I wrote letters to the Father in the name of Jesus. I was confident that the Holy Spirit was directing my thoughts and writings. I carefully penned meaningful Scriptures, inserting the names of loved ones. As I re-read the flowing words, I realized I was writing heartfelt prayers.

Later, I led a prayer group in which we worked together to find Scriptures that covered many prayer subjects and situations. These prayers evolved into the book series now known as the *Prayers That Avail Much Family Books.*

Throughout the years, I have received countless testimonies of how these prayers have given the new believer direction and the seasoned

Christian additional tools for uniting in prayer. Praying these prayers aloud also increases one's faith because faith comes by hearing and hearing by the Word of God. (Rom. 10:17.)

Praying the Word

Prayers That Avail Much is my story, the result of my relationship with the Heavenly Father and the practical application of God's Word to my everyday life.

You, too, can pray prayers that avail much. The Word of God is available to you. Not only does God speak to your heart from the pages of His written Word, but He also speaks to your inner being in a quiet voice.

At times, it seems God is feeding thoughts into your mind. You see, you are a partaker of His divine nature. And as you spend more time with Him, you become more like Him, conformed into His image by the Spirit of God.

In Ephesians 6:18 (AMP), we are instructed,

Pray at all times (on every occasion, in every season) in the Spirit, with all [manner of] prayer and entreaty. To that end keep alert and watch with strong purpose and perseverance, interceding in behalf of all the saints (God's consecrated people).

Prayer is not mystical, but practical and purposeful. Prayer is a spiritual business with written laws that govern the affairs of life. Prayer consists of different forms of supplication and entreaty.

As believers, we are to be alert and watch with strong purpose. *Our purpose is to enforce the triumphant victory of our Lord Jesus Christ here on earth.* We do that as we continually pray, "Father, Your will be done on earth as it is in heaven."

So don't ever give up; keep on persevering. The Holy Spirit is practical, and He leads you into the reality of all reality.

Praying scriptural prayers will change you from the inside out. Praying God's Word, which is truth, will cause you to become more willing to face reality and deal with the truth about yourself and your situations. It will also help you grow in the grace and knowledge of our Lord Jesus Christ.

As you replace your old thought patterns with God's thoughts, even your behavior will change. You will be transformed from the inside out, enabling others to see Jesus in you!

CHAPTER 2

Personal Growth Through Prayer

Jesus spoke these words in John 15:1-3 (NIV): "I am the true vine, and my Father is the gardener. He cuts off every branch in me that bears no fruit, while every branch that does bear fruit he prunes so that it will be even more fruitful. You are already clean because of the word I have spoken to you."

Over time I would come to understand these words.

At times, the realization of our own need for spiritual growth can be a stunning blow, jolting us out of a self-righteous stupor just when we least expect it. I remember one such occasion that caught me totally off guard.

I was ministering at a church on a particularly bright Sunday morning. The last amen had been said, and I walked down the steps to the main floor. I stood just in front of the podium to greet those who were streaming forward to speak with me or request prayer.

Many expressed their appreciation for my books, which had given them inspiration. I received warm handshakes, hugs and exclamations of "I've had your books for years. *Prayers That Avail Much* changed me completely. I feel as though I've known you all my life!"

Several shared brief testimonies with me. One joyful gentleman said, "I'm a Christian today because my wife started praying the prayer of salvation from your book for me. Thank you for your obedience!"

Then I became aware of her: a tall woman with noble features and a lovely face, which I suspected concealed her deepest feelings.

The woman introduced herself, and as we spoke, her eyes quickly welled up with tears. She explained, "I have prayed and prayed your prayers for my husband, but he hasn't changed. If anything, he's drinking more. The abuse hasn't stopped either. Why hasn't God answered my prayers? What am I supposed to do now?"

Sensing her heartache, I reached out, took her hand and drew her closer. I listened as she recounted her situation. It was obvious that she had been pushed to her limits. I longed to pray with her for the strength to redefine her boundaries.

I have found that when we are able to admit our powerlessness to change others, we are ready for God to open the eyes of our understanding. Then we can detach ourselves, in a healthy way, from those who have hurt us and step out of the emotional turmoil that keeps us unbalanced and off center. God restores our balance so that we can withstand Satan and be firm in our faith.

When one partner in a relationship changes in this way, that change often generates change in the other person. In fact, a small change in one's behavior can generate tremendous results. I thought to share these truths with the woman who stood before me. Perhaps her change would be the key to turning her situation around.

After validating her pain and expressing sympathy for her situation, I asked, "Can you share with me the transformation you have experienced? How have the prayers changed *you*?"

Her reaction was immediate. Instantly, her tears dried, and through clenched teeth she said, "I am *not* the one who needs changing!" With that she turned around briskly and walked away.

My heart ached for her as I prayed for God to reach this wounded heart with the truth that would set her free. What she did not realize was that God had given her the power to make decisions concerning her own life but that she wasn't responsible for her husband's behavior. Her feelings of frustration and perplexity could catapult her to another level of spiritual growth if she would focus her intense desire on knowing God instead of changing her husband.

The First Pruning

God is a loving Father, and He wants us to mature and become *reconcilers*—living witnesses to others. Many times when praying for others, we have an opportunity to be the link that will reconcile them to God *if* we are first willing to allow our own hearts to be changed in the process. Such change is seldom easy. But if we allow it, our lives will produce fruit that creates a desire and willingness to change in the hearts of those for whom we pray.

My encounter with the woman who was convinced that only her husband needed to change reminded me so much of myself a few years earlier. I could hear myself expressing a similar thought to God about my own husband.

In those early days when I began to read and study God's Word, I felt so special, so pure, so free and so perfect that I couldn't see any personal shortcomings or weaknesses in my own life. I was in for a rude awakening.

Jesus said, **I am the true vine, and My Father is the vinedresser** (John 15:1 NKJV). I understood that I was a branch of this true vine. What I didn't realize was that I had some attitudes that were like stray shoots (gardeners call them "suckers") that had to be cut away before I could be an effective channel of intercessory prayer.

The first wrong attitude the Vinedresser dealt with in me was self-righteousness. As soon as that attitude was exposed, the pruning process was set in motion.

Pruning is not painless, and it is not a one-time experience. But I am grateful for the Father's pruning process because it produces a harvest of rich fruit in the lives of those who will yield to the Vinedresser's hand.

When I spoke with the woman who was angry because her husband hadn't changed, I didn't realize that, to my chagrin, our encounter would provoke another pruning experience for me.

Although others continued to come up to the platform to speak with me or ask for prayer, my heart was heavy with grief for the woman who for a brief moment had revealed her hurt and anger. I rejoiced with those who rejoiced, but on the inside I wept for the woman who had walked away.

My brief encounter with her was the catalyst that thrust me into a new study of the grace of God and, as a result, another spiritual adventure. (I find that often when I pray for others, God performs another work of grace in me. For this I am very grateful.)

Growing in Grace

God's grace is difficult to define. Yes, it is unmerited favor, but I believe that it is far greater than intellectual knowledge can explain. We cannot fix its boundaries or determine its limits. God's grace is illimitable and available to all.

God saw you before you were born. Every day of your life was recorded and every moment laid out before a single day had passed.

Life comes from God, and in His mercy, He breathed into us the grace to survive in the outside world. Even as we were being formed in utter seclusion, woven together in the darkness of the womb, He understood the family situations and the social environment in which we would develop into men and women. His grace enables us to adapt and survive in a world foreign to spiritual beings.

God's grace is a supernatural element that comes down from above. This vital spiritual principle guides us to an encounter with truth. John says that when we acknowledge Jesus as the Son of God, He gives us grace for grace—*grace upon grace, full grace, grace heaped upon grace.* It seems that words are too general and insufficient when one speaks of "amazing grace!"

God's grace is an expansive ocean that you enter by faith. This region is a place of safety, and the fruit of grace is God's glory.

God's grace is a vital ingredient in the growth process that occurs in all of us. We are spiritual beings attempting to live in a natural environment, and the Word of God is our nourishment.

Self-improvement can help shape our character to a degree, but a sense of fulfillment will always stay just outside of reach. On the other hand, God's grace empowers us to invite Him thusly:

> **Investigate my life, O God, find out everything about me; cross-examine and test me, get a clear picture of what I'm about; see for yourself whether I've done anything wrong—then guide me on the road to eternal life.**
>
> **Psalm 139:23,24** THE MESSAGE

His examination of love brings fulfillment and a sense of well-being.

It is written, **Grow in grace, and in the knowledge of our Lord and Saviour Jesus Christ** (2 Peter 3:18). As you grow in grace, rejoicing in hope and enjoying the glory of God, you reap the fruit of emotional healing and spiritual growth. Your faith increases, and you become wiser and more attuned to God's will. The reward of your faith is the salvation of your soul, and you are able to share these fruits with others.

We cannot grow without experiencing pruning, and pruning is usually painful—a pain that leads to healing and greater victory. This, too, is God's grace. Truth, when spoken in love, makes us free. However, the truth sometimes hurts.

Admitting that I am at fault and that I have failed in my climb to perfection remains very difficult for me. But as I grow in God's grace, I am able to detect my shortcomings and recognize my condition as I carefully examine myself along with the loving scrutiny of my Heavenly Father. I know that my growth in God is not by works of righteousness but by His grace alone.

When I first began to grapple with changes in attitude, I wrote down appropriate Scriptures and then read them aloud. My affirmations of God's Word allowed me to grow in the fruit of the Spirit and achieve another level of maturity in Christ Jesus. God continued working in me so that my prayers availed much. More and more, I came to understand the truth of Proverbs 3:11-12 (THE MESSAGE):

> **But don't, dear friend, resent God's discipline; don't sulk under his loving correction. It's the child he loves that God corrects; a father's delight is behind all this.**

Corrected and Disciplined

My first serious encounter with God's correction and discipline is etched vividly in my mind. It was early morning as I sat down at one end of the sofa for my meeting with the Lord. After greeting the Father and acknowledging the presence of Jesus, I asked the Holy Spirit to take the things of Jesus and teach them to me. Opening my Bible to Matthew 18, I eagerly began to read.

Oh, I was so joyful, so delighted to be in the presence of the Trinity as verse 10 seemed to stand up in huge letters!

> **Beware that you do not despise or feel scornful toward or think little of one of these little ones, for I tell you that in heaven their angels always are in the presence of and look upon the face of My Father Who is in heaven.**
>
> **Matthew 18:10 AMP**

Immediately, my defenses were up. I thought of a thousands of justifications to assure me of my innocence: "God, You know I'm Your child, and I would never allow myself to despise one of Your little ones. How could I ever feel scornful toward anyone?"

So often we sugarcoat our wrong attitudes and bury our true feelings. However, when we continue to hide or deny the reality of our feelings in the face of apparent truth, it paralyzes our growth.

The Holy Spirit is the One who convicts and convinces us of sin, righteousness and judgment. So in His gentle way, He reminded me of the family's drive home after the previous Sunday morning service.

As the scene unfolded in my mind, I felt so ashamed. But I still wasn't ready to let go of my defense. I remembered how I had once again dissected our pastor's sermon, explaining where he was wrong. I could hear my husband's voice: "This man is a man of prayer who has been studying the Bible for at least twenty years, and you began studying only two or three years ago. How is it that you have learned more in two years than he has in twenty?"

Indignantly, I explained to my husband in a very firm voice that I had been studying longer than he knew anything about. God had called me to teach, and after all, I had received "revelation knowledge" of which he knew nothing. All this was for the benefit of our four children, who were sitting in the back seat. (God forgive me! To this day my children still dislike Sundays.)

At that time, I had very little experience in the school of prayer. So as I sat there on the couch, I continued my line of defense before the Lord, "Now, Holy Spirit, You must realize that I could not allow my children to believe what our pastor was preaching. After all, I am responsible for teaching them the truth."

Feeling that my defense was justified, I attempted to read on, but verse 10 would not let me go. The pain of having to admit my sin—despising and feeling scornful of one of my Father's children—was almost more than I could bear. The bottom line was that I had never resolved my issues with authority figures. My issue had to be clarified and unraveled.

My face burned with shame when I realized the effect my criticism was having on my children. It was painful for me to admit that my husband was right and I was wrong. How puffed up and self-righteous I sounded as Sunday after Sunday I criticized the pastor we had chosen for ourselves and our children! The entrance of God's Word exposed the darkness, and the pruning began as I confessed my sin.

> **He is faithful and just (true to His own nature and promises) and will forgive our sins [dismiss our lawlessness] and [continuously] cleanse us from all unrighteousness [everything not in conformity to His will in purpose, thought, and action].**
>
> 1 John 1:9 AMP

Overcoming Obstacles to Prayer

To walk in the Spirit is to walk in the light. To walk in the light is to walk in reality. The entrance of God's Word is light, causing our thoughts and purposes to be exposed, sifted, analyzed and judged. Selfish, self-centered thought patterns and attitudes are stripped away.

God's calling is sure; therefore, He must correct, discipline and prune us, for we are His channels of prayer. He knows us, and He wants us to know ourselves. Intercession must issue from a pure heart—not from a broken-down, wounded soul. Prayers offered out of our past hurts and unresolved issues miss the mark.

One of the greatest obstacles to growth in our relationship with God and man is denial. Denial is a defensive technique that enables us to function in the face of overwhelming circumstances. Often the shock of certain situations is more than our minds can absorb. Therefore, we simply do not see facts, even though everyone else can see the reality of all that surrounds us.

Denial is a useful shock absorber at times, but continuing in this state leads to delusion. Denial then becomes an enemy, opening the door to giants of addiction and compulsive, obsessive behavior.

Denial is a stronghold we need to pull down with spiritual weapons. The Spirit of Truth leads us into all reality. It is hazardous to our spiritual growth when we refuse to accept reality, acknowledge our sin and receive forgiveness. God has gone to great lengths to make provision for us through the blood of His Son: **The blood of Jesus Christ His Son cleanses (removes) us from all sin and guilt [keeps us cleansed from sin in all its forms and manifestations]** (1 John 1:7 AMP).

The life of God is a light that penetrates the darkness of denial and self-deception. The psalmist wrote, **The entrance of thy words giveth light.** (Ps. 119:130.)

Each time you speak God's Word as a prayer, He watches over His Word to perform it in you and on behalf of others. Your own spiritual walk then becomes an adventure, and you eventually realize that everyone must walk his individual pathway leading to the way, the truth and the life—the reality of knowing Jesus as Lord. The changes in you can influence others and give them hope.

Keep in mind that growth is gradual. Little by little, as we persevere in our pursuit of the grace and knowledge of God, we are able to conquer moral conflicts, agitating fears, insecurities, bad habits and unhealthy attitudes and behavior. The Holy Spirit is a gentle Guide and a tender, understanding Leader. As we grow in grace, we are able to face our fears and admit our shortcomings.

The Father is in charge of our growth rate. Our responsibility is just to cooperate with Him as He cleanses and prunes us that we might bear more fruit.

Another enemy to Christian growth is perfectionism. Perfectionism is a mental giant that either drives people to perform or discourages them from even trying. After attempting to climb the many ladders of perfectionism without success, some quit trying altogether.

I know from personal experience how perfectionism can render a person immobile until procrastination becomes a way of life. I learned to rely on someone to rescue me. Invariably, either a loved one or an employee would fill this role.

Procrastination can be an entrenched stronghold that does not want to let go. For example, a typical scene of procrastination in my life would look something like this: a speaking engagement is only a few days away, and I haven't prepared as I should. The everyday business of operating a ministry demands attention. Christmas is coming, birthdays are around the corner and there is much work to be done.

My friends are running around, getting everything together so they can enjoy the holidays. In the back of my mind, I know I should be praying, studying, making plans and preparing for my family, but other urgent things get in the way. Things begin to scream at me, and I continue to push them away. This procrastination interferes with my prayer life, causing the pressure to build.

In the past, procrastination relieved me of making decisions for which I would have to be accountable. Thus, the door was opened wide for others to make decisions for me—but usually not the decision I wanted.

Trapped in the very throes of procrastination, I was plagued by guilt. I felt I deserved all the condemnation anyone could heap on me. I had learned the importance of performing well in my early childhood, and I didn't want to be judged and found wanting. In spite of this, I was my own worst critic, inviting others to heap verbal abuse on me.

At this time, by the grace of God and the patience of my publisher, several of my books were on the market. Even though these books were successful, I could never enjoy the success as *my* success. Recognizing that procrastination was the cause of much stress and anxiety, not only for me but for others as well, I prayed diligently to overcome this problem.

Finally, God revealed to me in a vivid dream that the controlling fear at the root of my procrastination was the fear of both failure *and* success. Basically, I feared making a decision.

I couldn't bear the thought of making a decision that would fail. But I also feared making a decision that would lead to success. What if I couldn't sustain that success—then what? So I avoided either outcome by simply making no decision at all.

The Dream

I will never the forget the dream God gave me to expose that root of fear and set me totally free. That dream is as real to me today as it was a few years ago.

In the dream, I blurted out with frustration, "Oh, my goodness! I've done it again! Today is the birthday luncheon, and I don't have a gift." Jumping up, I hurriedly dressed, raced out the door to the car and drove to my favorite gift shop. Grateful that no other cars were on the road, I thanked God for helping me again. I did think it strange, however, when I didn't see any cars in the entire parking lot.

It was then that I realized all the stores were dark. Where was everyone? What was going on? Opening my car door, I realized that the parking lot was a sheet of ice. In fact, the entire place was covered in ice. *That's the reason no one is on the roads,* I reasoned. *Well, since I drove here, I guess I can drive back. No, on second thought, I think I'll walk back home very carefully.*

Again, I opened the car door to get out. As I looked behind me, I saw that the parking lot had turned into hills and valleys and each valley had become a pool of water. But I couldn't swim! How would I ever get to the road?

As I continued to contemplate my situation, some menacing figures appeared. They were all giants. One group was made up of teenagers with sneering grins, waiting for me to walk in front of them. There was no other way out; I had to pass by them. I was so afraid. Then a giant appeared at another interval. He was evil-looking and beckoned for me to come to him.

Finally, I had no choice. *If I remain here, I'll die,* I thought. There was no one to rescue me. No one knew where I was. I could take my chances and bluff my way through, but I still had no idea how I would cross the valleys of water or get past the giants.

Fearfully and carefully, I began walking. It was a pain-filled journey, but I had to go on. As I walked, one by one the hills were leveled, and as I approached the waters, I realized they were not overflowing. In fact, I didn't even get wet. The giants were still waiting, but my courage seemed to increase.

I approached the group of teenagers who were laughing at me. Then as I drew near within their reach, I realized they were just cardboard cutouts—nothing but paper dolls! The huge, menacing figures weren't even real.

God's grace was present; my courage increased, and I continued walking toward the evil-looking man who hadn't changed his posture. Lo and behold, he wasn't real either! He was just like the cutouts in movie theaters. Just then I awoke.

My prayers were becoming reality. God was at work in me, revealing my buried fears to help set me free.

It is by His grace that we go from one degree of glory to another. Any fear that holds us in chains must fall helplessly behind us when we acknowledge them in the light of God's Word.

I am learning to face situations for which I am responsible and make decisions. I am no longer afraid of failure or success, even though at times those old, familiar feelings attempt to pull me into procrastination.

Today I can accept responsibility for my decisions because the Spirit of Truth exposed and removed a hidden root of bondage in me. That bondage would have hindered not only my effectiveness in life, but also my effectiveness in prayer—primarily because prayer is a lifestyle.

Choose To Lose Self

The level of your prayer life will always correspond to the level of your spiritual development. As you grow spiritually, your prayer life will develop to different levels. Soulish, emotional prayers will give way to effectual prayers that issue from the heart of God revealed in you.

Effective prayers are not motivated by emotions but by the Spirit of God. Jesus said to His disciples,

I still have many things to tell you, but you can't handle them now. But when the Friend comes, the Spirit of the Truth, he will take you by the hand and guide you into all the truth there is.

John 16:12 (THE MESSAGE)

If we are to become effective as channels of intercessory prayer, we must lay aside our love for self and our desire for self-preservation. We must make the decision to love God more than we love ourselves or our own desires.

Jesus said that he who loses his life shall find it. (Matt. 10:39.) As we grow in grace and the Holy Spirit reveals more truth to us about ourselves, we have to make choices. God will not deliver us from ourselves. He performs His will in us as we submit to Him, but we must let go of those things that so easily beset us.

The correction may be painful, but it is exciting to experience the ministry of transformation administered by the Spirit. Prayer makes tremendous power available to us when we believe. And when we grow in confidence, our prayers make tremendous power available to others.

I am so thankful that God loves us enough to correct and discipline us, showing us where we are wrong. Our lives become the road God walks when we make a determined choice to be conformed to the counsel of His will.

Wounded Souls Give Satan Access

Satan cannot arbitrarily defeat the child of God. He must be given an opening. Usually, it is out of ignorance, but at times we give place to him.

So often we attempt to put on the whole armor of God while holding on to wrong attitudes and wrong thought patterns. Then we wonder why our armor isn't shielding us. When having done all, we take our stand, and Satan immediately looks for an open gateway to our lives. If we give him place, we are staggered by his fiery darts.

How do we give place to the devil? Obviously, disobedience, unforgiveness and other sins give the devil a wide opening in our lives. But damaged emotions, hidden agendas and unresolved issues—often carried over from childhood—can alter a person's perception of the Word of God. As a result, wrong perceptions of God's Word leave us vulnerable to the lying strategies of Satan.

I remember when I was taking my first baby steps of faith. Each new step was thrilling. I wanted the whole world to know and accept the understanding I had encountered.

At times, when I compared myself with others (which the Bible tells us is not wise), I thought that I alone knew truth. My childhood training groomed me to be very rigid. But a stronghold of rigidity is a hindrance to praying effectively and must be annihilated.

The legalism taught by my church and lived by in my home was so much a part of me, I couldn't see that I was still in its grip. It was frustrating to me when others didn't grasp the truth I shared with them. In my zeal, I attempted to force them to adapt to my personal level of knowledge and understanding.

As 1 Corinthians 8:1 says, a little knowledge puffs up. When seen through the eyes of a wounded spirit, knowledge of the truth can become twisted and misused for the purpose of manipulation and control of others.

Spiritual maturity doesn't develop overnight. Growth is a process; it progresses line upon line, precept upon precept, here a little, there a little.

I remember the days when I diligently prayed the love chapter, 1 Corinthians 13, for my husband. Meanwhile, unknown to me, I had not overcome a self-righteous attitude—an attitude honed and refined over the years of playing the role of *perfect* daughter. As a child, I was reminded almost daily, "Remember who you are. You are the pastor's daughter, and you must be a positive example to others." On the outside, I tried to reach perfection, while on the inside I despised being forced to play the role of "Miss Goody Two Shoes."

The enemy of our souls takes advantage of childhood experiences to trap us and defeat us before we are capable of evaluating what we are told by adults. In my case, I was singled out as the paragon, the model for my siblings and other children. I knew my imperfections, but I couldn't allow anyone else to see them.

Secretly, I believed I was a fraud. I was expected to act perfect, yet I well knew that I was not. As a result, I was filled with remorse and shame. I had no one to turn to with whom I could share my fears or sort out my feelings.

Through repetition, wrong thought patterns and attitudes can become so deeply entrenched that we cannot see truth. So, much to my sorrow, I continued to play this role—not only with people but also with God. I wanted to be His perfect daughter, and I actually thought I was!

I am so grateful that the Holy Spirit convicts us of sin, self-righteousness and judgment. He is faithful to lead us to repentance. Seeing my self-righteousness in the light of God's Word was revolting to me, and the thought that I would tolerate these "filthy rags" in my heart was almost more than I could bear. I repented with many tears and determined to change, reminding myself that I am what I am by the grace of God.

God is looking for availability, not perfectionism. He is able to use us as instruments of righteousness on a higher plane than our spiritual growth and understanding because it is Christ in us that makes the difference—*He* is our hope of glory.

Salvation of the soul is progressive, and it is experienced as we pray scripturally. Meditation on the Word of God becomes the engrafted Word written on the tablets of our hearts. God's Word divides asunder the spirit and soul, exposing our motives and giving light to live by. Our behavior changes as carnal mind-sets and attitudes give way to the righteousness of God.

Changing Me From the Inside Out

A wrong mind-set that Satan used as a gateway to my soul was my erroneous conviction that if my husband would change, if he would just "get it together" spiritually, then we could have the perfect marriage and become an example to others.

I was faithful in my praying. I prayed and confessed scriptural prayers over and over for my husband. To my amazement, the Holy Spirit led me along the pathway of emotional healing for myself, revealing past hurts and resentments that rendered me helpless and victimized in certain situations. I discovered that harbored hurts and resentments are both hindrances to praying prayers that avail much.

Symptoms of the wounded spirit I had never acknowledged were exposed in my relationships with others. The slightest hint from another person suggesting that I had been less than pleasing could send me into days of repentance and self-pity. I was an open receptacle for blame, guilt and condemnation. For me, the shame of being a disappointment to another person or to God was overwhelming and unbearable.

When something went wrong, I was sure it was my fault. It would take days of asking for forgiveness before I could function properly again. I was easily intimidated by real or imagined criticism. I understood when someone remarked, "One word of criticism can undo a hundred compliments."

My defense against real or imaginary rejection was simply to move into emotional isolation, withdrawing into the prayer closet. Thank God for the prayer closet! It was my salvation during those days of denial and ignorance concerning my own need for attitude changes.

The day came when I finally realized that what I prayed for others was not yet completed in me. God, who had started a good work, continued to transform me from the inside out. He exposed my wrong attitudes and mind-sets to help me come out of the wilderness of denial into reality. Suddenly, strongholds began to come down.

Inconsistencies revealed in my affirmations and behavior became clearer to me as I continued to pray the love chapter—no longer for my husband but for myself. The Word I prayed with my understanding became a healing tool in the Master's hand for my own life when I finally became willing for God to remove my shortcomings.

As difficult as it may be to accept, the truth is that when our prayers are not answered, it's time to check out our love walk. (1 John 3:21-24.) Much too often, we project our feelings onto others, not dealing with the personal hindrances that harass us. We see ourselves as perceptive, judging another's motive, yet we can't see the reality of pride and self-righteousness in our own lives.

In Matthew 7:3 (NIV), Jesus speaks of self-deception, asking, **"Why do you look at the speck of sawdust in your brother's eye and pay no attention to the plank in your own eye?"**

The prayers I had prayed for others began to develop in me. The process was not painless, but it led to the reality of victory in Jesus. Changes continue to take place—changes from the inside out.

Changed by the Power of God

If one is to live in the land of reality, one must speak truly, deal truly and live truly. (Eph. 4:15.) To do so takes a made-up mind, a simple commitment to self to do the right thing. This leads to having a greater commitment to others. It requires a decision to live according to Ephesians 4:22-24 (NKJV):

> **...that you put off, concerning your former conduct, the old man which grows corrupt according to the deceitful lusts, and be renewed in the spirit of your mind, and that you put on the new man which was created according to God, in true righteousness and holiness.**

This decision is a personal one, requiring a rejection of all falsity and childish mind games. The mind must be renewed or reprogrammed to the Word of God. The apostle Paul wrote about this process:

> **When I was a little child I talked and felt and thought like a little child. Now that I am a man I have finished with childish things.**
> **1 Corinthians 13:11** PHILLIPS

Prayer prepares us for life outside the prayer closet. As we put on the Lord Jesus Christ, our behavior changes. Instead of reacting to outside forces, we learn to take responsibility for our own actions and to allow others the freedom to be responsible for their personal growth and behavior.

When clothed in Christ, the person who acted out the role of the enabler faces truth and no longer excuses the inappropriate behavior of others. She is empowered by the Holy Spirit to be a living testimony of God's love, a witness to Him in her home and in her community.

The person who played the part of life's victim becomes more than a conqueror when she puts off the old nature and mind-set and puts on Christ. The one who was intimidated overcomes fear, and the child of darkness becomes a child of the light. Self-condemnation turns into self-evaluation as believers learn to overcome by the blood of the Lamb and the word of their testimony. (Rev. 12:11.)

Praying reflectively produces emotional healing and spiritual growth. It takes courage to be willing to change and reliance on the Holy Spirit to show you how to change.

When I listen to testimonies of men and women whose lives have been changed by the power of God, I am amazed at the different avenues they have walked.

For instance, one woman whose husband was addicted to pornography became convicted by the Holy Spirit that she could no longer live as her husband demanded. She shared her conviction and asked him to go with her for counseling.

However, the husband didn't want to give up his destructive activities. So she gave him a choice. When he realized that his wife's ultimatum was to go for counseling and give up his addiction or move out, he chose to leave.

This woman of God let her husband go. It wasn't easy, but she realized that, as a child of the light, she could no longer be a partaker of evil. She could no longer live a life that was displeasing to God.

Change produces change, but the change may not always be what we expect.

Prayer is not for the purpose of controlling a spouse, child, parent or friend. *The Message Bible* says God has given us the power to be our true selves. (John 1:12.)

Although we are responsible *to* others, we are not responsible *for* others' behavior. Therefore, we must determine where our responsibility ends and where that of another begins.

When we seek first the kingdom of God and His righteousness (His way of doing and being right), it frees us from the need to compare ourselves with others—a practice that produces confusion and complications. It is also human nature to want to change those closest to us for our own comfort. But when we walk in the light as He is in the light, we learn to make allowances for others.

Galatians 6:4-5 in *The Living Bible* states,

Let everyone be sure that he is doing his very best, for then he will have the personal satisfaction of work well done and won't need to compare himself with someone else. Each of us must bear some faults and burdens of his own. For none of us is perfect!

Every believer who genuinely desires growth must face the reality of his own imperfections and allow the Word of God to scrutinize his innermost being. One of the first lessons I learned is that I cannot change any other human by my own efforts. Only God and the individual produce change that endures.

'Strip Off' the Old
Before You 'Put On' the New

So often we get ahead of God, ultimately delaying our growth process in the Spirit. We are so eager to put on the new nature that we fail to strip off the old nature. Instead, we merely cover the former nature. However, this type of spiritual facade eventually falls.

The apostle Paul tells us what to do in Ephesians 4:22-24 (AMP):

Strip yourselves of your former nature [put off and discard your old unrenewed self] which characterized your previous manner of life and becomes corrupt through lusts and desires that spring from delusion; and be constantly renewed in the spirit of your mind [having a fresh mental and spiritual attitude], And put on the new nature (the regenerate self) created in God's image, [Godlike] in true righteousness and holiness.

My heart's cry has always been that I will stay well-balanced so I can endure. In the earliest stages of my prayer life, I had no understanding about "stripping" away my former nature, so I ignored that part and skipped down to "putting on" the new.

I can assure you from personal experience that when your heart is upright before God, He moves heaven and earth to answer your questions and give you understanding.

A few years ago, while driving down the highway near my home, I couldn't believe my overwhelming feelings of anger and confusion. "God," I prayed, "What's wrong with me? How dare I even think that I have anything spiritual to give to anyone? I cannot continue in the ministry unless You do something to change me!"

When I stopped whining, the Lord said, "I am ready to work into your being all that you have prayed to be established in others."

Well, I certainly didn't understand that. "God, I've been walking with You and confessing Your Word for years. You watch over Your Word to perform it in me. Give me an example of what You're saying."

God will talk with you when you are *ready* to hear. That day He said to me, "You have believed and confessed that I have not given you a spirit of fear, and I haven't. But there is a phase in My program you have missed. It's time to face the fears you have. You have forgotten a past that has not forgotten you."

Even though I had experienced many changes in my life and had avoided overt sins, I had no understanding of the covert sins that kept me bound—strongholds of rigidity, emotional isolation, denial and silence.

Oh yes, I understood that we are not to live by the letter of the law but by the Spirit. But when severe, painful obstacles arose, I became more rigid about keeping to the letter of the law and expected everyone around me to do the same.

Walking in love was my great quest and aim in life. But in times of stress, I'd lose control, and old behavior patterns would crop up. Then I'd spend days repenting "in sackcloth and ashes."

So God began to help me strip away, put off and discard of my old unrenewed self. This was the beginning of a painful but rewarding new life.

We have to put off the old before we can successfully "put on" the new man—the new self. The soul doesn't want to give up its control, but as the mind is renewed day by day, our souls are restored to new life.

Very often we begin in the ministry with good intentions, desiring to please God in all things. We know that man shall not live by bread alone but by every word that proceeds from the mouth of God. (Matt. 4:4.)

But we become so busy doing God's work that we neglect personal time with our Father. We even avoid Scriptures that annoy us and grab hold of Scriptures that we believe support our new freedom.

When past hurts remain unhealed and unresolved issues hinder us from making godly decisions, our egos get in the way of our walking in the Spirit. Circumstances become too uncomfortable, so we revert to and reinforce our former strongholds that helped us survive past situations that were beyond our control. At that point, these strongholds become fortresses to hold us prisoner and keep God locked out.

But God doesn't give up on us! Jesus continues to stand at the door and knock, and when we open the door, He comes in. In His presence, there is understanding, healing and restoration, for He forgives us and restores our souls.

Do you need to change your mind-set or behavior? Wait on God's plan. Don't run out ahead of Him. He knows when you are ready to proceed with the next phase of spiritual growth.

Someone said, "It's better to have God wait on us than to have to wait for God to clean up our mess." In other words, it's better to learn to pray before personal crises instead of *in the middle* of them.

Healthy Relationships
Within the Church

To effectively participate in the various forms of prayer, it is imperative that we keep our hearts pure and approach God with clean hands. This requires us to walk in love, forgiving one another and stripping away resentment. It is impossible to pray effectively for others when we harbor a judgmental and critical attitude toward them. Our self-righteousness is repulsive to our loving Father. Fear also prevents us from resolving issues.

James tells us to pray for one another:

> **Confess to one another therefore your faults (your slips, your false steps, your offenses, your sins) and pray [also] for one another, that you may be healed and restored [to a spiritual tone of mind and heart].**
>
> **James 5:16 AMP**

This theme is woven throughout the book of James.

The Scriptures reveal the importance of healthy relationships within the church. God chooses men and women—apostles, prophets, evangelists, pastors and teachers—to

> **...equip God's people to do his work and build up the church, the body of Christ, until we come to such unity in our faith and knowledge of God's Son that we will be mature and full grown in the Lord, measuring up to the full stature of Christ.**
>
> **Ephesians 4:12-13 NLT**

In our relationship with God, we learn His ways. The Holy Spirit teaches us how to live every day—in the privacy of our homes, in the business world and in the church. We can develop a lifestyle that honors God as we obey 1 John 1:7 (NLT):

If we are living in the light of God's presence, just as Christ is, then we have fellowship with each other, and the blood of Jesus, his Son, cleanses us from every sin.

As God's children, we learn to lead lives worthy of our calling, for it is God who has chosen us, called us and equipped us. We grow in grace and in the knowledge of our Lord Jesus Christ, assuming responsibility as His children.

Through true fellowship with God, we learn to develop healthy relationships with one another, to honor and prefer one another in love. We also learn how to **think of ways to encourage one another to outbursts of love and good deeds** (Heb. 10:24 NLT).

In healthy relationships, we give each other room to grow, making allowances for our humanness. We avoid emotional entanglements, recognizing our respective rights—the right to say no without defense.

Confessing Our Faults to One Another

Why can't we keep our weaknesses private, a secret known only to God? The essential ingredient in the life of the believer is agape love—a love that is greater than all our sin, a love that is greater than the sins of those for whom we are praying.

Loving others as Christ has commanded does involve human connections. As our lives are revealed, this closeness to others often exposes certain weaknesses and personality flaws in our dispositions.

The desire of most who live a life of prayer is to walk honestly before God. Confessing our sins and revealing ourselves to our heavenly Father and to other human beings allows us to live uprightly before God and man.

The question is, can we humbly face ourselves with an accepting, nurturing and forgiving attitude? Can we take responsibility for our behavior? Are we afraid of not being accepted just as we are?

Yes, our new nature allows us to walk in newness of life as we keep ourselves in the love of God that has been shed abroad in our hearts. His grace gives us the ability to make choices. But we must be patient with ourselves and with others as **the Lord's searchlight penetrates the human spirit, exposing every hidden motive** (Prov. 20:27 NLT). *The Living Bible* refers to "the Lord's searchlight" as **a man's conscience.**

The maturing believer takes responsibility for his attitudes and behavior. He deals truly, speaks truly and lives truly in good relationship with himself, with God and with others. He is a doer of the Word, not merely a hearer.

Sometimes we find ourselves in uncomfortable places. God desires for us to be in harmony with each other and to do no evil to anyone:

> **Do things in such a way that everyone can see you are honorable.**
> **Do your part to live in peace with everyone, as much as possible.**
> **Romans 12:17-18** NLT

God is our shield and our defender. With the Spirit of Truth as our Helper, we can risk revealing our weaknesses. We can walk into a place of liberty, free of all fear. Even Jesus selected certain ones to be His inner circles of friends. He is our example, and we can safely follow Him.

At one time or another, everyone has felt the sting of betrayal when a confession shared in confidence was divulged. I remember a time when my words were countered against my good intentions. Since that time of crisis, I have learned to pray and became discriminatory when choosing those with whom I share my weaknesses and shortcomings.

So pray on every occasion that you would walk in wisdom and discernment and be led by the Holy Spirit in your choice of confidants. You must know that you are in a safe place, hidden from the strife of tongues.

The benefits of a God-selected confidant are a true blessing and offer considerable healing and consolation. A bonding of spirits often results in heartfelt tears and expressions such as, "You have just described my life!" Acceptance such as this leads to prayer wherein both individuals may be healed and restored to a spiritual tone of mind and heart.

Truly, the confidence of being able to bear your burdens and troublesome moral conflicts with someone in prayer avails much. This venture of revealing weaknesses appropriately promotes honesty, wisdom, discernment, prudence and freedom.

The Eternal Effects of Prayer

The individual whose heart is upright toward God and man will find over a period of time that praying for others results in personal healing, restoration and spiritual growth. As James 5:16 (AMP) says, **The earnest (heartfelt, continued) prayer of a righteous man makes tremendous power available [dynamic in its working].**

This same power that is at work in us is released on behalf of those for whom we pray. As transformation takes place in us as individuals, the lives of others are also affected because change produces change. Our prayers prepare the way for others to see truth and experience deliverance, salvation and transformation.

We are accountable to one another. We who believe are carefully joined together, becoming a holy temple for the Lord. (Eph. 2:21 NLT.) Praying for one another is called intercessory prayer. No one is exempt from needing prayer. Prayer that is sincere and honest, lacking condemnation and judgment, is powerful in its ability to heal and restore believers to soundness and well-being—spirit, soul and body.

As we become more deeply and intimately acquainted with the Father, we learn to walk in love with one another. The two intercessors who cannot fail—Jesus and the Holy Spirit—know us even better than we know ourselves.

The Holy Spirit intercedes for us without condemning us. Jesus neither accuses nor condemns us before the Father. He is the One who died and was raised to life for us and now is sitting at the place of highest honor next to God, pleading for us. (Rom. 8:33,34; Heb. 7:25 LBT.)

By God's grace, let us follow His example. Let us mend the broken-hearted and lift up the bowed down. Let us live lives that offer healing and be instruments of reconciliation, conformed fully to the character and nature of Christ.

CHAPTER 3

What Is Prayer?

I want men everywhere to lift up holy hands in prayer, without anger or disputing.

1 Tim. 2:8 NIV

Most Christians readily agree that prayer is something they should do. Those who pray usually say they should pray more. Many acknowledge a desire to pray but cite their lack of time or lack of ability as reasons for their prayerlessness.

When people say they don't have time to pray or they don't know how to pray, it is clear that they don't understand what prayer is.

What is prayer? Simply put, prayer is talking with God. Prayer is communication with the Supreme Being who has promised to show you things to come. (John 16:13.) Prayer is a privilege that releases the promises of God to become reality in the life of the one praying or in the lives of those for whom we pray.

Our prayers are limited only by His promises, and He has given us great and exceeding promises. Our confidence in God is rooted in knowing Him and His will.

'Pray What You Know To Pray'

A few years ago, God had to remind me of the simplicity of this particular truth. I was at home that day and the house was quiet, but I was angry with myself for my lack of productivity. Everything seemed to be a struggle that day—my writing, my reading and especially my praying. Out of frustration, I shouted to God, "What do You want? I don't know how to pray or what to pray. What do You want me to do?" The gentle voice of the Holy Spirit spoke to my heart, *Do what you know to do. Pray what you know to pray.*

The answer seemed so simple and easy. I reached for *Prayers That Avail Much* and began to pray. I came to the Master with all my imperfections, fell down at His feet and prayed the way He had taught me to pray so long ago.

God wants us to come to Him in prayer just as we are. Effectual prayer is learned by praying. As we talk with God, we develop a love relationship with the Creator of the universe. As we practice prayer, our desire grows to know more of God. That desire to know Him is a response to His calling us to a higher plane and deeper depths.

Actually, at one time or another, everyone prays. Even when we did not know God, we called out to a Supreme Being for help. When we felt the most out of control, we wanted to believe that Someone greater than ourselves would come to our rescue.

Prayer takes on new meaning when we become children of God. We enter into a relationship with the Supreme Being, who is also our Father. He loves us unconditionally and will provide for us completely.

What is prayer? E. M. Bounds wrote,

> Prayer is a divine arrangement in the moral government of God, designed for the benefit of men, intended as a means for furthering the interest of His cause on earth, and carrying out His gracious purposes in redemption and providence.[1]

I like to think of prayer as a conversation between God and man. God has spoken in words that we can read, and He sent a Teacher who gives us spiritual understanding.

The Bible is God's speaking to His children. In this manner, He shares Himself with us so we can become more deeply and intimately acquainted with Him. When we share our thoughts and ourselves with God, we call it prayer. Prayer becomes a love relationship between God and man.

Prayer Is a Lifestyle

Prayer isn't something a person *does;* it is something he *lives.* Prayer evolves out of a study of the Scriptures and personal fellowship with the Father. The true believer is motivated by a desire to please God. This is the desire that the apostle Paul so eloquently expressed as his ultimate goal: **I want to know Christ and the power of his resurrection and the fellowship of sharing in his sufferings, becoming like him in his death** (Phil. 3:10 NIV).

Praying for others emerges out of a heart of love for the Father. Peter wrote,

> **Knowing God leads to self-control. Self-control leads to patient endurance, and patient endurance leads to godliness. Godliness leads to love for other Christians, and finally you will grow to have genuine love for everyone.**
>
> **1 Peter 1:6,7 NLTB**

Praying for others is an act of compassion that issues from the recreated human spirit. One of the ways we serve God and others is by the means of prayers, including intercessions, supplications, petitions and the giving of thanks. We are to pray about everything and for everyone in accordance with 1 Timothy 2:1-4.

When you submit yourself to God as a channel of prayer, He will give you prayer assignments from His heart to yours. Prayer assignments, identified at times as "burdens," may be long-term or short-term.

Jesus is seated at the right hand of the Father praying in the heavens. We, as members of His body, are His channels of prayer in the earth. And the Holy Spirit, who knows the mind of God, is our Helper in the task.

It seems that some believers have been given a special measure of grace to pray on behalf of those who cannot or will not go to the throne of grace in prayer. However, prayer is not an activity reserved for a select group of people. James, who according to tradition was the brother of Jesus, issued the directive to everyone: **Pray for one another, that you may be healed. The effective, fervent prayer of a righteous man avails much** (James 5:16 NKJV).

James gives us assurance that the prayers of the righteous will be effectual. In James 5:17, he relates the story of the prophet Elijah, an Old Testament character who was a human being with feelings, affections and a constitution like ours. When this man stood before the God of Israel, his prayers released extraordinary power.

Likewise, when we who are in Christ Jesus offer heartfelt, continued prayer, tremendous power is made available and is dynamic in its working. (James 5:16 AMP.) Heartfelt prayer produces results, or answers.

The foundation for answered prayer is faith. Without faith, it is impossible to please God. (Heb. 11:6.) We receive a measure of faith when we are born again that develops through the different levels of spiritual growth.

However, much too often our prayers lack substance. Prayers without substance are like clouds without water. We find ourselves praying words that fall to the ground, and we go away disappointed. Our confidence is shaken. Why? Because prayer becomes merely a form of godliness without power. The focus has been diverted from "God, our Father, hallowed be Your Name" to the act of prayer itself. But the call from God is to stand in the gap before *Him*.

In the body of Christ, there are many misconceptions concerning prayer. One hindrance I have witnessed among prayer groups when they come to stand before God in prayer is that far too much time is spent fighting a defeated foe. Other times, a false sense of responsibility for another person's behavior motivates believers' prayers. As a result, they attempt to impose their will on a person rather than praying according to the will and plan of God for that person.

This latter misconception about prayer is most often a problem when we are praying for family members. It is human nature to want to change those closest to us for our own comfort. But that desire is born of selfishness, not the love of God. The God-kind of love has a different response:

**Let everyone be sure that he is doing his very best, for then
he will have the personal satisfaction of work well done and won't**

need to compare himself with someone else. Each of us must bear some faults and burdens of his own. For none of us is perfect!

Galatians 6:4,5 TLB

A needy person may become preoccupied with the power of prayer, believing that God has sent him to save an entire congregation or ministry. He may think that he alone has heard from God, so he attaches himself to a prayer group for the purpose of enlisting others in his call to pray. A person like this is usually sincere, so when he senses opposition, he either retreats behind emotional walls of isolation or moves to another group, seeking a place of acceptance and leadership.

The church is God's family on earth. Therefore, we are mutually dependent one upon the other. We need everyone to take his ordained position of ministry.

Each believer is important to the body of Christ. God isn't willing that any should perish. For this reason, He has designed His body to allow and require each joint to supply and support the other. One way in which that supply is released is through prayer.

Praying for One Another

The church is to pray for one another. God looks for those on earth who are willing to bridge the gap for others, to rebuild the broken-down walls and to take a protective stance before Him, "making up the hedge," as it states in Ezekiel 22:30.

In this passage of Scripture, we read that the walls of Jerusalem were in disrepair. Today, our "wall" is in disrepair as long as there are factions and division in the body of Christ. The wall represents faithful people committed to God, united in their efforts to resist evil. These lively stones are those who will turn others back to God.

The gaps in the wall represent those who use their religious dogmas, philosophies and reasoning to whitewash sin. They cover sin over with compromise instead of cleaning it out with the Word.

At times, I have looked for Scriptures that would justify my belief system, only to find out later that what I believed was wrong.

You see, God will move heaven and earth to reveal truth to us when we desire to walk after the Spirit and not after the flesh. Therefore, we are to pray for all saints, because we are one body and one Spirit, and God lives in us all. When one member falters, the stronger members will support him and lift him up.

When we pray for the lost, we enter into the ministry of intercession by taking our position in Christ at the right hand of the Father. We then join with Jesus, our intercessor, to pray for the new convert to be conformed to the image of Christ. Jesus, who remains a Priest forever, is therefore able to save everyone who comes to God through Him. He lives forever to plead with God on their behalf. (Heb. 7:24,25 LBT.)

As we take our place in intercession, we allow His ministry to be expressed through us on the earth. In truth, we all need someone who loves us enough to pray until Christ be formed in us. (Gal. 4:19.)

As members of the body of Christ, we must be equipped to do God's work and build up the church. (Eph. 4:11,12.) Therefore, we need the ministry of divinely appointed apostles, prophets, evangelists, pastors and teachers to teach, lead and guide us. We also need knowledgeable intercessors, willing to enforce the triumphant victory of Jesus Christ on behalf of others.

We who have been given the measure of grace to pray for others must consistently guard against missing the mark in our eagerness to do something for God. We must be cautious not to throw around too many thus-says-the-Lords in our attempts to help Him out. We cannot afford to run ahead into spiritual warfare without learning the basic principles for personal growth.

I believe that Paul's letter to the Ephesians designates prayer as a lifestyle and was written to equip the church to walk in the Spirit. Walking in love, in the light and in wisdom establishes within us the character we need to be prepared for the spiritual warfare of the believer.

In chapter 2, we dealt with personal growth through prayer. Many believers are unaware of the personal growth process outlined in the book of Ephesians. Instead, they try to psychologically strategize and outmaneuver the enemy. As a result, they become wounded individuals within the hallowed walls of the church. Why? Because they attempted to stand against the devil while walking in the vanity of their minds.

Paul's epistle to the Ephesians changed my life and is today my favorite book on prayer. I believe that the first five chapters introduce and lead up to Ephesians 6:10 (NIV), which says, **Finally, be strong in the Lord and in his mighty power.** With this verse, Paul expresses the climactic purpose of the entire book, which is a call to intimacy with God through prayer.

Throughout history, books have chronicled the lives of men and women who purposed to pray. Many famous ministers, prayer warriors themselves, have credited the success of their ministries to these precious men and women who remained in the background.

Who were these men and women who spent their lives praying? Did they achieve such power in prayer because they had reached a higher level of maturity? Were they more spiritual than other believers? Did they instinctively become experienced intercessors overnight, or was there a learning and maturing process?

An intercessor must release his need to control others. He must also resist the temptation to "fix" others in an attempt to prove that his prayers avail much.

It is imperative that as intercessors we remain flexible in the hands of the potter, allowing Him to perform in us that which we are believing Him to do in others. As we intercede, God is continually at work in us, assisting and helping us to work out our own salvation with fear and trembling. (Phil. 2:12.)

Our response and degree of submission to God's Word governs the maturity process. The Word planted in our hearts brings about the personal salvation of our souls—which is defined as the mind, will and emotions.

God does not wait for us to become perfect before He works through us to bless others. In fact, no matter where we are in our process of spiritual refinement and emotional healing and development, He will use us if we are willing vessels. God is looking for availability. Wherever we might be in our spiritual development, we are able to comfort those who are in any trouble by the same comfort with which we ourselves are comforted by God. (2 Cor.1:4.)

If we are to present our bodies a living sacrifice, holy and acceptable unto God, as our reasonable service, it will require a renewing of our minds. (Rom. 12:1,2.) Our thought patterns must be changed from conformity to the world system to obedience to God.

God desires that we see ourselves through His eyes. This transformation comes about through honest introspection, rather than through dogmatic condemnation wrapped up in the fabric of "religion."

God wants us to understand who we are in Christ, the individuality of our own personality and the interdependence He planned among all of us in the body of Christ.

He views us as His very own children. He rejoices over us with love, looking past our imperfections and flaws. He lavishes wisdom and understanding on us, that we might enjoy the blessings He has already provided. And for the good of the entire body of Christ, He causes us to become a supporting ligament, assuming our place of responsibility in love. (Rom. 12:5; 2 Cor. 6:18; Eph. 1:4; Zeph. 3:17; Eph. 4:16.)

Without continued emotional and spiritual development, we never experience the full blessings of God. We remain in a state of immaturity, living on spiritual milk—still infants who are not acquainted with the meat of righteousness. (1 Cor. 3:1-3.)

Knowledge alone will not develop the nature of God within us. We must seek after wisdom and understanding, which includes common sense and good judgment. These virtues enable us to appropriate God's Word in our everyday lifestyle.

> **Getting wisdom is the most important thing you can do! And with your wisdom, develop common sense and good judgment.**
>
> **Proverbs 4:7 TLB**

In Colossians 1:9 (AMP), Paul prayed that we might **be filled with the full (deep and clear) knowledge of His will in all spiritual wisdom... and in understanding and discernment of spiritual things.** So along with knowledge and wisdom, let us get understanding and discernment: for revealing truth through self-awareness, for the strengthening of our faith and for the development of a practical and productive life.

Hebrews 4:12 (AMP) tells us where to go to obtain the wisdom, understanding and discernment we need:

> **For the Word that God speaks [and His Word that we speak] is alive and full of power [making it active, operative, energizing, and effective]; it is sharper than any two-edged sword, penetrating to the dividing line of the breath of life (soul) and [the immortal] spirit.**
>
> **Heb. 4:12 AMP**

To pray scriptural prayers is to pray the Word that God has spoken. This form of prayer keeps us alert to detect anything that might hinder us.

Identification

You may find it difficult at times to know where your emotions end and someone else's begins. In retrospect, I know that many times my emotions and the reality of another person's emotional hurt and wounds got mixed up with the workings of the Holy Spirit, who desires to teach us the dividing line of soul and spirit.

It was early in my days of learning to pray for others that I first experienced the phenomenon of identification through intimacy and communication with God. I had been praying for an individual who was under great pressure. He was experiencing emotional pain from the conflicting influences surrounding him. This turmoil was preventing him from making crucial decisions about his future.

During a particular intercessory prayer session, I began to feel uncomfortable. A sense of confusion was followed by a sweeping depression. I quickly jumped up from my place of prayer, interpreting my emotional reactions to spiritual prompting as an attack from the enemy against me personally.

Yet I knew I hadn't completed my prayer assignment, so I continued to seek God for answers. How could the enemy jump on me when I was in prayer? Was there a scriptural explanation for this occurrence?

Later, I realized that my lack of knowledge and my emotional reaction had opened the door to frustration and discouragement and had paralyzed my desire to pray. After all, it had only been a short time since I had experienced a wonderful personal deliverance from anger, confusion and depression into light and liberty.

Satan used my wrong perceptions about his abilities to deceive me into believing that when I prayed for others to be delivered, I would become a victim. He wanted me to believe that as I enforced the triumphant victory of Jesus against his demonic forces, these defeated foes would be able to overcome and defeat me.

That is completely untrue. We are overcomers by the blood of the Lamb and the word of our testimony. (Rev. 12:11.) Jesus is Lord over the spirit, soul *and* body!

Often I am asked, "Aren't you afraid to engage in spiritual warfare? After all, you know, the devil might turn and jump on you with the very demons and spirits you are attacking." Satan might attempt to pressure you into believing that lie, but you just have to declare in faith, "It is written...."

The enemy of our salvation cannot arbitrarily jump on anyone. He has to have a gateway opened to him by wrong thought patterns and wrong religious dogmas. Paul says we are not to be ignorant concerning Satan's devices. We are to give no place to the devil! The choice is ours.

The Holy Spirit is faithful to lead us into all reality. He taught me that my feelings could not be classified as good or bad and that I could decide whether to respond or react. God never intended for my emotions to control me, so I have learned to subject my emotions to the control of the Holy Spirit.

So when you face difficulties in the midst of praying for others, take a moment of time in prayer to determine your response. You can choose to press on through to victory regardless of your feelings, or you can allow your feelings to govern and defeat you in your prayer life. Establish your identification in Christ, and thus determine the benefit of your influence.

If God is for us, who can be against us? (Rom. 8:31.) We are God's instruments, His channels of prayer.

The Word of God divides the soul and the spirit. As you practice scriptural prayer and develop an intimacy with God, you learn to distinguish the promptings of the Holy Spirit from your own emotions. You also begin to understand God's purpose for the insight He is giving you.

As you continually acknowledge the Holy Spirit as your Helper in prayer, He will give you understanding. There are times when He will reveal a person's struggle and you actually will experience the emotion of that person's turmoil and pain. This identification is the beginning of God's plan for you to enforce the triumphant victory of Jesus against the forces of darkness so deliverance can come to someone caught in a trap of the enemy.

Self-deception is the bane of the believer, and pride is the veil that blinds the eyes of the unbeliever or backslider. (2 Cor. 4:3,4.) Such are the strongholds we are commissioned to resist and remove:

> **It is true that I am an ordinary, weak human being, but I don't use human plans and methods to win my battles. I use**

God's mighty weapons, not those made by men, to knock down the devil's strongholds.

These weapons can break down every proud argument against God and every wall that can be built to keep men from finding him. With these weapons I can capture rebels and bring them back to God and change them into men whose hearts' desire is obedience to Christ.

2 Corinthians 10:3-5 TLB

Before someone can be born again or restored to fellowship, the strongholds—every proud argument against God and every wall that can be built to keep men from finding Him—must be destroyed and demolished. Our weapons of warfare are mighty through God to the pulling down of these strongholds of pride and self-deception.

After the Holy Spirit gave me insight, I resumed my place in prayer on behalf of the young man who was unable to make crucial decisions affecting his future. I was touched with the feelings of his infirmities, but now I was able to bypass my own emotional involvement, which Satan had earlier used to divert attention from my prayer assignment to myself. By the grace of God, I focused once again on yielding to the Holy Spirit so the intercession of Jesus—who was touched with the feeling of the young man's infirmities—could flow through me.

It is imperative that we hold close to our own hearts the feelings, intents and purposes of the Father's heart. This is what enables us to connect spiritually. In other words, we must come into agreement with the intercession of Jesus, for praying out of the desire of His heart is what creates prayers that avail much. (1 Cor. 2:16.)

This young man later shared his experience of deliverance with me. The light of the gospel opened his eyes and pierced his heart. The confusion, anger and depression that had rendered him powerless to make a decision was exposed, and the darkness became light.

Through prayer, you can tap into the spiritual realm. It is imperative that you crush your own strongholds and renew your mind to the Word of truth. Then Satan will be thwarted in his attempt to distract you, for he will have nothing to latch on to in order to pull you off course in prayer.

You have been given power and authority over all the power of the enemy. When you walk after the Spirit, you learn to resist the temptation of reacting emotionally to rebel spirits that would oppose you in prayer. You are the church, and the gates of hell cannot prevail against you as you determine to enforce the triumphant victory of Jesus against the forces of destruction on behalf of others.

Truth Lights Your Way

According to *The Message Bible* in Ephesians 5:14, **The bright light of Christ makes your way plain.** Knowing and understanding that truth will make your way clear and light up your prayer life.

Prayer is doing business with God. Therefore, the ability to separate soulish emotions from spiritual leading is crucial to praying effectually.

Some believe that the more emotions displayed in prayer, the greater the anointing. Godly wisdom is given to you to understand the difference between your emotional feelings, the feelings of others and the prompting of the Holy Spirit. So when praying for others, take the time to discern your true feelings, allowing the Word of God to divide between the soul and the spirit.

For whatever God says to us is full of living power: it is sharper than the sharpest dagger, cutting swift and deep into our innermost thoughts and desires with all their parts, exposing us for what we really are.

He knows about everyone, everywhere. Everything about us is bare and wide open to the all-seeing eyes of our living God; nothing can be hidden from him to whom we must explain all that we have done.

Hebrews 4:12 TLB

God knows what is in our spirits. He is looking for that one who is available to pray. He brings us together in the spirit, connecting our intercession with that of Jesus.

You will not have to go on "witch hunts" that produce shame, fear and self-condemnation. You can rely on God. He is faithful to correct misconceptions, to discipline us as sons and daughters and to heal our damaged emotions as we respond to Him.

Often when we continue to perceive demonic activity or a self-defeating attitude in another, it is actually God's prompting for us to look at ourselves. How much easier it is to project onto others the change that God desires to work in our own souls! So when we think we perceive an ungodly attitude in the one for whom we are praying, the opportunity to examine ourselves is at hand.

Guard against transferring or projecting onto others personal feelings and attitudes that God is seeking to transform in you. Sometimes it is more comfortable to see that speck in your brother's eye than the plank that is in your own eye. It is spiritually and emotionally jolting when you face facts that require you to change your mind-set and behavior.

Our first reaction to change is usually resistance, but we must remember: obedience is better than sacrifice. (1 Sam. 15:22.) Change produces change. Healing and growth become a living reality when we surrender to needful change.

As we approach God our Father with a spirit of humility, we need to remain open to the Spirit of Truth who uncovers, exposes and enables us to resolve both overt and covert sin. (John 16:8,13.) Unresolved anger and unidentified damaged emotions are often hindrances to our prayers.

When we don't see the results for which we are longing, we tend to pressure those closest to us to change, even though we are unable to change ourselves. But it isn't discussion that destroys strongholds. We demolish the strongholds of others after we have brought our own thoughts into obedience to Christ.

Be alert in prayer! Pray scriptural prayers, submitting to the loving scrutiny of the Holy Spirit. Examine yourself! Ask yourself, *Have I moved over into spiritual pride? Am I praying for others in order to increase my sense of self-worth? Have I fallen into the trap of self-righteousness, believing that God has called me to correct and change others?*

Prayer is intimacy with a loving Father who leads you into complete discovery and development of your personality. Praying for others may fulfill a need to be needed, but never neglect the responsibility for your own attitudes and behavior. It is easy to avoid responsibility for yourself by trying to control the attitudes and change the behavior of others if they are disturbing your personal comfort level.

Be willing to deal truly, speak truly and live truly with yourself, with God and with others. Open the door of your heart for godly self-evaluation and unobstructed communion with God.

Be sensitive to the reality of your own needs, and acknowledge the provision of the Good Shepherd. In Him you shall not lack fulfillment. He supplies and fills to the full your every need, whether financial, social, emotional, mental or spiritual.

You are laying down your life when you are willing to pray for others and to be touched with the feelings of their infirmities. It requires you to set aside your own agenda, displacing the strong desire to have things your own way.

Jesus is the intercessor seated at the right hand of the Father with whom we unite in His present-day ministry. As He is, so are we in this world. The church is His voice in this earthly realm as we submit to the Lordship of Jesus.

Our prayer life will take on new life, and more power will be released when we deny self by taking up our cross and following Jesus. (Mark 10:21.) Jesus said, **"Anyone who wants to follow me must put aside his own desires and conveniences and carry his cross with him every day and keep close to me!"** (Luke 9:23 TLB).

Prayer for one another is essential to the well-being of the church. Individually, each one determines to lose his life so he may find it.

When you come to Jesus, you determine to listen to Him. Jesus said that whoever loses his life for Jesus' sake will save it but whoever insists on keeping his life will lose it: **"If your first concern is to look after yourself, you'll never find yourself. But if you forget about yourself and look to me, you'll find both yourself and me"** (Matt. 10:39 THE MESSAGE.)

How do I lose my life? By the grace of God, I use the weapons of my warfare and pull down strongholds, casting down imaginations and every high and lofty idea that exalts itself above the Word of God. (2 Cor. 10:4,5.) I pull down rigidity—my tendency to insist that my methods are right and everyone else's are wrong—and submit to the ministry of transformation by the Holy Spirit.

I pull down walls of emotional isolation and learn to guard my heart with all diligence, trusting in the love of God. I ask Him to remove the places of hardness and fill them with His love. I embrace the compassion of Jesus for others and pull down the strongholds that hinder me from understanding truth. I give up my own reputation, count the cost of serving God and walk by faith in Him. I lose my life so I can find life—and that life is more abundant!

My prayers for others avail more and more as I maintain my focus. They become more powerful and effective as my confidence and faith in God becomes established in quietness and assurance. With the weapons of my warfare, I pull down judgmental and critical attitudes that might be holding others in bondage. From this stance, victory is assured.

"Let God arise and His enemies be scattered!" is my triumphant declaration. My fervent plea is "In my life, Lord, be glorified." My anthem is "To God be the glory—great things He has done!"

Prayer Is Talking With God

Moses knew the ways of God. He was not afraid to reveal his disappointments, frustrations, anger and fears to the God in whose presence he dwelled. David who wrote many of the Psalms, expressed his innermost thoughts to Jehovah God even while declaring his trust in Him. In Lamentations 3:17, another prophet named Jeremiah expressed his true feelings of despair. This opened the door for him to receive hope and confidence.

You can talk openly with God—your wonderful Counselor, your Prince of Peace—about anything. Tell Him your innermost thoughts; describe your fondest dreams; expose your true feelings, desires, wants and needs; express your love and gratitude to Him with thanksgiving. It may be possible to hide your true feelings from others or even from yourself, but it is impossible to hide your feelings from God.

Often feelings are a barometer, alerting us to a need for change in our thought life. Unfortunately, we sometimes misuse the Scriptures as a cover-up for a feeling we perceive as "wrong" instead of acknowledging the feeling and expecting answers from the Lord to determine the cause and the remedy.

But God is concerned about everything that concerns you. (Ps. 138:8.) Ask Him for what you believe you need. Allow Him the time to speak to you and to show you your *real* need.

> [God's] **compassion never ends. It is only the Lord's mercies that have kept us from complete destruction. Great is his faithfulness; his loving-kindness begins afresh each day.**
>
> **Lamentations 3:22,23** TLB

The psalmist David would talk to himself during times of discouragement: **Why am I discouraged? Why so sad?** Then he would declare his trust in God: **I will put my hope in God! I will praise Him again—my Savior and my God!** (Psalm 42:11 NLT).

Praise God for answered prayer and for your victories and successes. Then thank Him for all He has provided for you. He created you, He understands you and He can "fix" you when you submit to His instruction. He takes the sting out of your hurts, dissolves your toxic shame and gives you the grace to overcome your fears and failures.

God desires to meet with you, to hear your voice and to see your face before Him. So come into the Holy of Holies and receive His love, His healing, His mercy and His grace. Great is His faithfulness!

God can be trusted with your secrets. He will never betray you. He is the God who hears you and answers prayer.

When you acknowledge your hurt or pain, you are able to receive healing and restoration. His grace enables you to forgive those who have harmed you and to forgive yourself for harming others, allowing you to make amends when necessary. You are able to comfort others with the comfort you have received.

This kind of honesty with ourselves and with God enables us, with the assistance of the Holy Spirit, to clear out emotional interference to an effective prayer life. David understood this when he prayed:

Who can discern his errors? Forgive my hidden faults. Keep your servant also from willful sins; may they not rule over me. Then will I be blameless, innocent of great transgression.

Psalm 19:12,13 NIV

It is the blood of Jesus that washes us and cleanses us. As we proclaim scriptural prayers over our own lives and the lives of others, the Word of God creates in us a pure heart, renews a steadfast spirit within us, restores to us the joy of His salvation and grants us a willing spirit to sustain us. Then we are able to teach transgressors His ways, and sinners will turn back to Him. (Ps. 51:7-13.)

God will not allow anyone to control or manipulate another person's will. But when we are in right fellowship with God and with others, our prayers bring people to the place of truth where they can receive the motivating knowledge to make a decision on their own. We are colaborers with God, and He involves us in His plan of salvation as His instruments of righteousness to pray for His will to be done.

Developing a consistent prayer life is an adventure in faith. God is very practical, and He has reserved specific pathways of prayer for you to walk as you become more deeply and intimately acquainted with Him.

You will have experiences as you move from one degree of glory to another. However, be careful not to seek sensationalism or attempt to reproduce in the flesh the experiences you had in the Spirit. Seeking experiences opens the door for demonic activity fabricated by familiar spirits. These spirits use our misguided thought patterns to keep us unbalanced and prevent us from pursuing an intimate relationship with God our Father.

One of our greatest temptations is to place God in a box. We want Him to answer our prayers in the exact manner He did previously. How we love formulas with steps 1, 2 and 3! But we must never forget that God is a multi-faceted God. He answers prayer in His own way and in His timing.

We often insist that God do things at our level of understanding when He wants to lead us to higher heights and deeper depths. Demanding that He perform His works exactly as He did in our last encounter with Him hinders our spiritual development and cuts off answers to our prayers.

Our God knows every aspect of every situation, and He continually desires to teach us His higher thoughts and ways.

Experiences in Prayer

It is amazing how God will direct and navigate our paths according to His higher ways when we ask and trust Him to lead us into His will. The Holy Spirit leads in subtle, unsensational ways. Yet His subtle, insistent prompting will always guide us to the supernatural direction and provision of God for our lives.

Years ago, I was preparing to attend a Bible study one day when the weather outside was not particularly inviting. I wanted to remain indoors with a good book and my cup of coffee, but I couldn't because the ladies would arrive soon for the Bible study. I couldn't just stay home because, after all, I was the teacher. So I dressed, collected my things and with umbrella in hand, I hurried through the cold and rain to the car.

After the last amen, we dismissed the meeting. I could hardly wait to get home. I was already relishing the thought of changing into something comfortable and crawling into bed for a nap before the children arrived home from school.

As I approached the intersection near a friend's house, I was impressed to stop in for a visit. After arguing inwardly for a few moments, I realized that even if I ignored the Holy Spirit's prompting and went home, I would not be at peace.

As I pulled into my friend's driveway, I noticed that she had a visitor. It seemed appropriate to back out and go on my way, but the prompting to see my friend would not go away. I had learned the consequences of disobeying God too many times to ignore His leading. So in spite of my feelings, I parked the car and once again stepped out into the rain.

That day I met a lady at my friend's house who could hardly talk for sobbing. She had been a Christian for many years and had recently become thirsty and hungry for more of God. In her search, she'd had a strange experience: She spoke in a language unknown to her and began to weep with groans that could not be expressed in articulate speech.

Others in her prayer group who had never seen anything like this began casting out "demons," calling upon God for her deliverance. She was most confused by their actions and reactions.

"How could the devil move in on me like this when all I wanted was to know God?" she asked. "Could it be that I have committed the unpardonable sin? Is something dreadfully wrong with me?"

Listening to the woman's story, I was excited that I had obeyed God's prompting to come to my friend's house. My friend and I then opened the Scriptures to this woman concerning Jesus, the baptizer, of whom John the Baptist said, **He shall baptize you with the Holy Ghost, and with fire**

(Matt. 3:11). As the three of us read from Luke 11:11-13, John 7:37-39, Romans 8 and 1 Corinthians 12 and 14, the Holy Spirit opened the eyes of the woman's understanding.

Up until that day, my time with God had been spent in personal study and fellowship. I was consumed with Him, and His Word consumed me. I had written countless letters and prayers to God, meticulously copying His Word as His promise to me. But this was the beginning of focusing my attention on intercessory prayer.

This dear lady became my first prayer partner. She prayed "with her spirit," and I prayed "with my understanding." Together we prayed and searched the Bible for answers, asking the Holy Spirit to remove from us any aura of mysticism.

God is so faithful! The Holy Spirit began to teach us, and we became aware of movements in prayer. It was as though we would catch hold of a particular need for prayer and stay with it, riding out the wave until we sensed a release. Sometimes we ended with exuberant rejoicing; other times the sweet presence of God would settle upon us, and we'd sit quietly, surrounded by peace.

Regardless of the type or expression of prayer, God graciously confirmed our prayers, as we saw yokes destroyed and bondages broken off the lives of those for whom we prayed.

Yield your entire being to be consumed with a fervent desire to prayer until the Spirit Himself takes hold together with you. For, as E. M. Bounds wrote: "It is only when the whole heart is gripped with the passion of prayer that the life-giving fire descends, for none but the earnest man gets access to the ear of God; and that is the purpose of prayer."[2]

Pray in Agreement With God's Will

P rayer is manifested in various forms. It is imperative that our prayers place us in agreement with God. We establish agreement with the Lord by articulating His Word.

First Timothy 2:1-2 lists an order of prayer that, when followed, assures us of a quiet and peaceable life:

> **I exhort therefore, that, first of all, supplications, prayers, intercessions, and giving of thanks, be made for all men; for kings, and for all that are in authority; that we may lead a quiet and peaceable life in all godliness and honesty.**

As God's colaborers, we are involved in His dealings with mankind. So in the name of Jesus, we approach God in faith and confidence. Taking our position in Christ, we address the Father in familiar but respectful conversational language, asking that His will be done on earth as it is in heaven. When we ask anything according to His will, He hears us. (1 John 5:14,15.)

In order to know God's ways and His will, it is imperative that we study to show ourselves approved unto God, workmen that need not be ashamed, rightly dividing the Word of truth. (2 Tim. 2:15.) God's will is revealed in His Word—so His Word *is* His will.

Our confidence in God is strong when we know what He says about the situations for which we are praying. He has given us the mind of Christ that we might comprehend His thoughts, feelings and purposes. As we study the written Word, we grow in the grace and the knowledge of our Lord and Savior Jesus Christ. We meditate upon the Scriptures, and our minds are renewed to a higher level of spirituality.

Out of our innermost being flow rivers of living waters. Thus, our prayers find their way into the desert places as the crystal springs of life overflow and make the waste places fertile. Our prayers become the very wings on which the answers already determined in the realm of the spirit are delivered.

Prayer is entering into agreement with the will of the Father. Our prayers released from this earthly realm make way for His will to be done here where we live out our daily lives.

Another confidence-builder is to approach the throne of grace with clean hands and a pure heart:

> **And, beloved, if our consciences (our hearts) do not accuse us [if they do not make us feel guilty and condemn us], we have confidence (complete assurance and boldness) before God, and we receive from Him whatever we ask.**
>
> 1 John 3:21,22 AMP

We are to lay aside every weight that would distract us from the heavenly vision. Hebrews 12:1 (AMP) defines *weight* as an **encumbrance (unnecessary weight) and that sin which so readily (deftly and cleverly) clings to and entangles us.** Weights are in direct opposition to the heavenly vision, which 1 John 3:2-3 (AMP) defines as the day we see Jesus:

> **...we shall see Him just as He [really] is. And everyone who has this hope [resting] on Him cleanses (purifies) himself just as He is pure (chaste, undefiled, guiltless).**

Praying God's Will for the Lost

Sitting in Sunday school class one day, I was astonished to hear someone ask, "How are we to pray for our unsaved loved ones? Is it God's will that everyone be saved?"

To know what God has said about mankind is to know His will. What does God say about mankind? First Timothy 2:4 (NIV) reveals that God's desire is for all men to be saved and to come into the full knowledge of the truth. This is our confidence and our assurance—that God will hear us when we pray for those who do not know Him. Knowing His will gives us the assurance that:

- The Lord of the harvest hears our prayer. (1 John 5:14.)

- He will send forth laborers into His harvest fields who will share the good news of the gospel with those who are estranged from God. (Matt. 9:38.)

- Those who hear and believe will be delivered from the authority of darkness and translated into the kingdom of God's dear Son. (Col. 1:13.)

The believer prays for the eyes of the spiritually blinded to be opened and flooded with the light of the gospel. Second Corinthians 4:3-6 (NKJV) states:

> **But even if our gospel is veiled, it is veiled to those who are perishing, whose minds the god of this age has blinded, who do not believe, lest the light of the gospel of the glory of Christ, who is the image of God, should shine on them.**
>
> **For we do not preach ourselves, but Christ Jesus the Lord, and ourselves your bondservants for Jesus' sake. For it is the God who commanded light to shine out of darkness, who has shone in our hearts to give the light of the knowledge of the glory of God in the face of Jesus Christ.**

After we have prayed for all men to be saved, we then pray the following prayer for our political and spiritual leaders in authority over us:

> *Father, I intercede in behalf of those in positions of authority, seeking Your intervention in the affairs of life. Thank You for spiritual leaders who tend, nurture, guard and guide us. We follow them as they follow Christ.*
>
> *Father, there is no authority except by Your permission. It is my prayer that the uncompromisingly righteous be in authority in our country so that the people may rejoice. May their offices be established and be made secure by righteousness. In the name of Jesus. Amen.*

Great benefits come to us when we pray with understanding according to God's will. This is the form of prayer Paul writes about in 1 Corinthians

14:15 when he says, **I will pray with the understanding.** We are to pray with all manner of prayer on every occasion and in every season. (Eph. 6:18; 1 Tim. 2:1.)

Prayer Presents the Case of Another

Prayer is a spiritual business. One day as I was praying for someone, I saw myself sitting at the end of a conference table. At the other end of the table was a man, and at my right hand sat another gentleman. The Holy Spirit spoke to my heart, saying that we were presenting a case to the Father and the Son.

"Where are you going to sit?" I asked. His reply was most comforting: *Here with you. We will present the case together.*

The Holy Spirit helps us when we don't know how to proceed. He directs our negotiations in the light of God's Word so that we can present another person's case to God for His consideration and divine intervention.

Praying for Troubled Marriages

In our ministry, we receive many prayer requests from individuals who ask us to pray for their marriages. For instance, we hear from defeated, down-trodden women who continue to live in abusive situations because they know that God hates divorce—and the church often reinforces this belief.

Such women ask us to pray specifically for God to make their spouses give up alcohol, drugs or the girlfriends or boyfriends with whom they are living. However, these are outward symptoms of both an emotional and spiritual problem. These wives want the marriage partner back home, but few ever count the cost. The illusion is "If he returns, I'll make sure everything is different, and we'll live happily ever after."

So many women fear being alone. It's difficult for these women to let go of their dream of the perfect marriage.

Years ago, during my first days of receiving prayer requests, I prayed diligently for every marriage to be saved. What a noble prayer. After all, a restored marriage would be evidence that our prayers were working!

God will speak to us by His Spirit if we will listen. At times, it is difficult for us to hear Him because we are rigid in our beliefs and insist on His doing things our way.

The day came when I met with a couple and attempted to apply the necessary pressure to put the marriage back together again. It was a "humpty dumpty" situation, but I was convinced that prayer would fix it.

But when what you are doing isn't working, it's time to seek God. Jesus said, "Seek and you shall find." (Matt. 7:7.)

Driving home that day, I cried out, "God, I no longer know how to pray. What is the problem here? What are we doing wrong?"

As I reviewed the hour the three of us had spent together, I observed in retrospect that the husband was a man who switched from hot to cold, from tenderness to hardness. When he spoke directly to me, gentleness controlled his conversation. Then, he would address his wife in cold, harsh tones.

"God," I prayed, "You can turn his heart toward his wife. We have prayed, and we want to see Your salvation in this marriage. You hate divorce, and You cannot permit our prayers to fail! But Father, forgive me for insisting on what I thought was right based on my limited understanding and not the full counsel of Your will. Not my will, but Your will be done."

Now, God hates divorce and marital separation, but that is not the end of what He says about it. God also hates **him who covers his garment [his wife] with violence. Therefore keep a watch upon your spirit [that it may be controlled by My Spirit], that you deal not treacherously and faithlessly [with your marriage mate]** (Malachi 2:16 AMP).

I realized that time would prove the extent of this husband's infidelity and deceit.

God allows divorce today for the same reason He allowed it in Moses' day—because of "hardness of heart." God has not called you to an abusive lifestyle. In spite of religious dogma, an emotionally or physically abusive marriage is not your cross to bear. You do have a choice. God has called you to peace. (1 Cor. 7:15.)

When we pray for a marriage, we often do not have the whole picture. The agreement of both husband and wife is required for a marriage to remain intact and to prosper.

I have witnessed many wonderful testimonies of restored marriages. When a spouse returns home, this can be the beginning of individual changes in both partners.

It isn't easy to change old behavior patterns, but it is necessary if we desire the fulfillment of our dreams. Old thought patterns, old defense techniques and old behaviors will produce the same old results. Sometimes answered prayer is costly. Are we willing to pay the price?

When praying for marriages, we bind the mind, will and emotions of each partner to the will of God, the plan of God and the mind of Christ. We encourage the spouse who is requesting prayer to let go of all religious doctrines and preconceived ideas and to allow God to work everything according to the counsel of His own will.

Satan began his attack on the woman in the book of Genesis. Even today, many women believe they have no choice but to live with abuse and oppression. When we advise women to take a stand for truth and right-eousness, their fear of being alone can be overwhelming.

Although it isn't easy, you can and must purpose to look beyond the temporal world and set your mind on those things that are eternal. Such a transition is a wonderful opportunity to pray and wait for the guidance of the Holy Spirit, who helps you when you do not know how to pray. According to John 16:13, He will show you things to come.

When praying for God's guidance concerning a troubled marriage, present your petitions to the Father according to His will and not according to your self-will. Don't ignore your feelings of rejection and betrayal, but know that God's grace is more than enough to heal you. He will enable you to stand your ground. So present your case to the Father, believing for His will to be done.

The Holy Spirit Reveals the Mind of the Father

Paul wrote, **I will pray with the spirit, and I will pray with the understanding also** (1 Cor. 14:15). A wonderful manner of prayer is returning God's Words to Him in articulate, comprehensible speech.

Many times when praying, the Holy Spirit will communicate certain Scriptures that apply to the circumstances. He reveals the intercession of Jesus as He continues His ministry of intercession at the right hand of the Father. (Heb. 7:25.)

How does God speak to us, and how do we recognize His voice? To receive anything from God, we have to believe that He is and that He is a rewarder of those who diligently seek Him. (Heb. 11:6.) In other words, we must receive from God by faith.

God is a master communicator. He designed us with the capability to listen to and recognize His voice: **For who among men knows the thoughts of a man except the man's spirit within him?** (1 Cor. 2:11 NIV).

Paul continues in this chapter: **Even so no one knows the things of God except the Spirit of God** (1 Cor. 2:11 NKJV). God is willing to reveal Himself to His people. We are colaborers with Him in prayer, and we make room for His participation and leadership. The Holy Spirit communicates to our spirits the very thoughts, intents and purposes of God's heart.

We cannot intellectually know God. His Spirit must dwell in us so we can begin to receive the knowledge of Him through revelation. The Holy Spirit from within reveals the mind of the Father to us. His ways are higher than our ways and His thoughts are beyond human understanding unless His Spirit discloses them to us. (Isa. 55:9.)

When God gives us a promise supported by Scripture, we may rest assured that we have the answer. The problem arises when we don't receive the promise or answer we desire. In the face of every challenge or controversy, we must say, "I bind the outcome of this situation and the will of everyone involved in this decision to the will, purpose and plan of God. I loose this situation from every curse and every device of the enemy. Thank You, Father, that Your will is accomplished in the name of Jesus."

God's Word will not return empty or void but will accomplish that which He desires. (Isa. 55:11.) All His promises are yes and amen in Christ! (2 Cor. 1:20.)

The Father Himself Loves You

If our earthly father was austere and emotionally isolated, it may be difficult for us to understand that God wants to be closer to us than that. We may remember learning early—when we were still small and so happy to see our daddy—that it wasn't acceptable behavior to run to him and try to jump onto his lap. We wanted the big hugs, but they were never offered. And our hugs were refused.

God is a "Daddy" whose heart's desire is to bless you. He longs for you to become more intimately acquainted with Him through seasons of prayer, meditation and the study of His Word. He wants you to know His will in all circumstances. Most of all, He wants you to know *Him*. Why? Jesus said, **For the Father Himself [tenderly] loves you because you have loved Me and have believed that I came out from the Father** (John 16:27 AMP).

Personal Prayer Experiences

Praying for the Father's goodness and love to draw a rebellious loved one to repent can challenge our faith and weary our patience. But if our fellowship with the Father is strong, we will remain confident and emerge with the desire of our heart granted. This was the case in the testimony of Rose.

The past weeks were very stressful, but Rose maintained her solid front of joy. She prayed that the light in her eyes would cause the hearts of others to rejoice. Throughout the course of each day, she prayed for her son's deliverance from drugs and from evil companions. She longed to see him awake to righteousness. As often as possible, she shared her concerns, her love and even the prayers she was praying for him. In the face of his scoffing and sneering, she rejoiced.

Rose believed that God would cause even his expulsion from school to work for her son's good. The next day at the beauty salon while sitting under the dryer, God spoke to her: *Go home when you leave here.* Deciding to obey, she drove home and walked into the living room. There she began to pray, declaring her confidence in God and proclaiming her love for Him.

As Rose prayed, she became aware that in the spirit she was sitting in a big lap with arms around her, holding her close. It was a safe place—warm, strengthening and comforting. At last she was experiencing something she had longed for all her life—the loving arms of a daddy, her loving heavenly Father.

Rose became quiet and calm, just resting. Not wanting to open her eyes, she longed to remain there in that room forever, held securely in the arms of God.

So often Rose had run into the throne room, boldly made her requests known unto God and then rushed out without waiting to hear His voice. But that morning Rose enjoyed a long, intimate conversation with God. She later was filled with joy when her full expectation was realized in the deliverance of her son.

The Father is always attentive to us, ready to extend His love. But are we listening to Him? Do we hear His voice speaking? If we listen, we will hear Him say, *All is well. Trust Me to work all things together into a plan greater than your dreams or imagination.*

One aspect of meditation is to wait before God and listen for His voice. In times of meditation we listen, reflect and visualize. What we hear depends on our willingness to pay attention to the witness of the Holy Spirit within us.

We learn from Joshua and King David to meditate in God's Word day and night. (Josh. 1:8; Ps. 1:2.) Meditative, quiet moments prepare us to hear His voice, even at moments when we least expect it.

God is not limited to quiet times to speak to us. However, it is in the times we appoint specifically to spend with Him that we are readied to hear His voice during our rushed and busy hours. I like to prepare for the day that is dawning in the early morning hours before the world around me is stirring.

My mother, Donnis Griffin, was a woman of prayer. After my dad retired, she asked God to give her a time when she could be alone with Him. She later told me, "Now, if you don't want the answer, don't ask."

She had always been a night person and had cherished sleeping late— much later than my dad. But the Holy Spirit said, *When Buck gets up to go jogging, you get up for our time together.*

"Oh, Holy Spirit, that's so early. He leaves at five o'clock in the morning!" But after pausing for a moment, she said quietly, "Oh, yes, I did ask, and You answered."

At bedtime that very night, she asked my dad to awaken her before he left the house for his morning jog. That was the first and last time he had to call her.

Ask the Holy Spirit to direct your schedule, and determine to obey His instruction.

Make an Appointment With God

Time alone with God is more vital to your well-being than eating. During these quiet times, read the Word, contemplate what you have read and write down your prayers. I find it helpful and edifying to keep a prayer journal. Writing in this manner and praying aloud accentuates the reality of the presence of God. This is also a wonderful opportunity to listen to praise and worship tapes.

Make a standing appointment with God. Take the time to start each day with quiet meditation. God will reveal Himself to you, and He will also give you direction for the day. The Holy Spirit will remind you of certain responsibilities, help you establish priorities and teach you how to pursue peace with everyone as much as it is possible with you.

He may remind you of a simple everyday task that needs attention. It may be something that is not important to you but *is* important to your spouse. God knows what you need to do to keep peace in your household, and He wants to be involved in your schedule. He is concerned about everything that concerns you.

As I wait upon the Lord, I sometimes visualize Jesus walking toward me in a beautiful green meadow beside a stream of crystal-clear water. Gentle breezes blow, invigorating and refreshing me. Jesus always approaches me with outstretched arms, inviting me to walk with Him.

At other times I visualize myself standing in a beautiful palace, bowing before the throne of God. The Holy Spirit is always at my side, prompting me, giving me the words to speak. Sometimes I see myself sitting at a conference table with the Godhead, planning and making my petitions known to Him.

God breathes the incense of your prayers. Your presence delights Him. And your petitions honor Him because you have acknowledged His power and willingness to help you.

During such times of meditation, endearing inner thoughts come to you. Learn to recognize the voice of the Good Shepherd. Meditate on God's Word. Listen to the spoken Word. His voice and His Word agree. Offer His Word to Him as a prayer, or simply rest, awaiting future revelation.

Pray in the Spirit as an act of your will to pray divine mysteries; then ask for the interpretation. This takes time, but as you practice the presence of God, you will learn the value of recording His messages to you.

His voice may come as an impression or an idea. Unless you are consciously meditating, sometimes you may think that it is your own thought process at work.

God not only speaks to us in the quiet moments; He also talks to us as we go about performing the everyday tasks of life. God will continue to claim your attention, however gently. He may pursue you with a thought—impressing you to read certain Scriptures and to pray scriptural prayers. He may present a particular need for prayer from His heart to yours. When you are attuned to God, you will recognize when He is calling you to pray for someone who concerns Him.

For instance, a person from the past may come to you in a mental picture or by name. Most often these prayers for others are intended as divine secrets between you and God. At times I feel led to call or write the individual with a Scripture or a word of encouragement that always points him or her to Jesus.

We do not know how a person should apply a Scripture or a word of encouragement to his situation. Therefore, it is wise to avoid interpreting for others what God is saying to them. Jesus is their Master. He alone knows every aspect of their need. He is the One who will confirm His Word and will to their spirit in His own timing and way.

Times of confirmation are most precious. God may confirm His voice through a Sunday morning sermon or a teaching tape, in the words of a song or during a conversation with someone.

One of my favorite (and I believe the most reliable) ways to be assured of having heard God's voice is through confirmation in the Scriptures. The Bible is a revelation of how God thinks about life and of His will for us. Not only does God speak to us by His Spirit, but He also speaks through His Word.

Therefore, the more time we spend in God's Word, the more familiar we become with the voice of His Spirit through that Word. Consequently, we become better equipped through study of God's Word to recognize His voice when He brings guidance or revelation to us in prayer.

Recognizing God's Voice in Prayer

When my four children were small, the six of us lived in a tiny frame house with a postage stamp-sized bathroom. The smallness of the room reminded me of hiding away in the secret place of the Most High. (Ps. 91:1.) I felt safe and alone with God there.

At the time, it had only been a few months since my encounter with God in my kitchen. One day the older children were at school, and the baby was taking her morning nap. As I leaned over the minuscule basin to wash my hair, anxiety over a teaching I'd heard kept intruding into my peaceful meditation.

I began complaining to God about what I considered to be erroneous teaching. After a while, I felt quietness supplanting my thoughts. While the water cascaded over my head, I "heard" a voice say, *Germaine, you do not have to fret and build a defense to protect my Word. I watch over my Word to perform it.*

I was eager to confirm the message. Previously, in my immaturity, I had received other impressions that proved not to be God but the thoughts of my own natural reasoning and thoughts that the devil had tried to inflict upon me. Having heard other voices floating up from inside me, I did not want to be deceived again.

I speedily rinsed my hair, turned off the faucet and tied a towel around my head. Dashing to the telephone, I dialed my dad, who was my spiritual mentor, and related my experience. "Is there anything in the Bible to support these words?" I questioned.

When I gave my father a chance to speak, he cleared his throat and said, "Yes, read the first chapter of Jeremiah."

After saying goodbye to my dad, I placed the receiver back in its cradle and reached for the white Bible I had recently purchased with s & H Green Stamps. There it was in black and white: **...for I am alert and active, watching over My word to perform it** (Jer. 1:12 AMP). I had heard the voice of God!

Before We Call, He Answers

God may even speak to you in the nighttime through dreams. I recall a dream He gave me in which I saw myself reaching for the telephone to call the doctor for my husband's grandmother. Before I could dial, three gentlemen appeared at my side. In amazement I said, "You came before I called!"

It was not until I opened my Bible the next morning that I even remembered the dream. The words seem to leap off the page: **Before they call, I will answer** (Isa. 65:24).

Day by day, month by month and year by year, your confidence will grow as God reveals Himself to you. The thought that the Creator talks with human beings is astounding to me to this day.

God talked directly to Moses, giving him instruction. He wanted to speak directly to all of Israel, but when He did, they were afraid and stood afar from Him. They asked Moses to talk to God for them, and they removed themselves from His presence. But according to Hebrews 12:18,22-24 (NKJV), we are not to respond to God's voice as the Israelites did:

> **For you have not come to the mountain that may be touched and that burned with fire.... But you have come to Mount Zion and to the city of the living God, the heavenly Jerusalem, to an innumerable company of angels, to the general assembly and church of the firstborn who are registered in heaven, to God the Judge of all, to the spirits of just men made perfect, to Jesus the**

Mediator of the new covenant, and to the blood of sprinkling that speaks better things than that of Abel.

God gives you the capacity to hear from Him. You will learn to appreciate this privilege more and more.

The Holy Spirit is a marvelous teacher. He will teach you how to pray effectively with your understanding as you carefully follow after Him and heed His instructions, reading the Scriptures and praying them aloud for yourself and others. In this way, you will develop a lifestyle of prayer, communing with God heart to heart.

In my earliest days of learning to pray, I prayed only with my understanding; I did not pray in the spirit. Everyone may not pray in a heavenly prayer language. However, this phenomenon of speaking directly to God in an unknown language is available to anyone who asks.

Even though I had grown up in a Pentecostal church, I did not know the reason for or the significance of praying words that I could not comprehend. I did not know that praying in the Spirit is a spiritual tool for speaking mysteries known only to God and that it would become an essential part of my prayer life.

Today I am so thankful that my introduction to prayer was praying God's Word aloud, inserting the names of those for whom I was praying.

Faith comes by hearing. As you pray the Word aloud, your faith is strengthened. Creative forces are released, and by God's grace, vistas of supernatural insight enable you to see everlasting, invisible things. (2 Cor. 4:18.)

The articulate words we speak in our prayer closet can be spirit and life, setting the captives free. On the other hand, our words can reinforce resistance in others if our motives are self-satisfying. It is God Himself who will bring about effectual prayers as we delight ourselves in Him. Faithful is He who called, who will also do it as we pray with our understanding and with the Spirit.

Praying in the Spirit

Many people have never experienced the depth of this second phase of prayer. "Praying in the Spirit" is a spiritual activity that helps us maintain life in God. When we pray in the Spirit, we are speaking mysteries, talking directly from our spirits to God.

Jude revealed one of the personal benefits of praying in the Spirit:

But you, beloved, building yourselves up on your most holy faith, praying in the Holy Spirit, keep yourselves in the love of God, looking for the mercy of our Lord Jesus Christ unto eternal life.

Jude 20,21 NKJV

This is why praying in the Spirit is such a useful tool for discovering God's plan as He imparts it to us. In the early stages as we begin to take necessary steps to fulfill God's plan, the vision may extend beyond our own faith level. But as we pray in the spirit, we are continuously building ourselves up on our most holy faith until the vision becomes possible and our mental excuses are cast down and overcome.

The Spirit of God energizes you to run with the vision God has given. So write the vision and make it plain. (Hab. 2:2.) Accept God's appointed time for the fulfillment of the vision, and be patient. It will surely come to pass!

Has God imparted a vision to you? In the beginning, visions can be very exciting. But your faith is tested when all the work begins and the details have to be formulated.

Sometimes it seems God asks us to extend our faith and believe Him for the impossible. We may be tempted to offer many excuses for not fulfilling our God-ordained destiny: "I'm too young." Or "I'm too old." "I can't speak before a group." "I don't have the proper education." "My spouse won't let me." "I'm too little—who listens to short people?" "I'm too big—who listens to people with a weight problem?" "I don't have a degree." "Where would the money come from?" The excuses we offer to God go on and on.

But when God gives you a vision, He also gives you the grace that enables you to fulfill that vision. That is why it's so important to pray both with your understanding and in the Spirit. When you pray the Scriptures, faith comes to you for the vision God has given you. And when you pray in the Spirit, your faith is built up sufficiently to act on what God has spoken to your heart.

So speak those divine mysteries in the Spirit, and believe that God is giving you the understanding, the ideas, the concepts and the insight to cooperate with Him in fulfilling His plan. A spirit of excellence will enable you to run your race in a manner that pleases God.

When you don't know how to pray or what to pray for, pray in the Spirit—it is a guarantee that you are praying the will of God.

> **Likewise the Spirit also helps in our weaknesses. For we do not know what we should pray for as we ought, but the Spirit Himself makes intercession for us with groanings which cannot be uttered.**
> **Now He who searches the hearts knows what the mind of the Spirit is, because He makes intercession for the saints according to the will of God. And we know that all things work together for good to those who love God, to those who are the called according to His purpose.**
>
> **Romans 8:26,27 NKJV**

When you are bewildered about how to pray for someone, that is an appropriate time to use your prayer language to pray in a tongue unknown to your natural mind. You may have exhausted your conscious knowledge of a situation, but there is still Someone who knows every aspect of the case. He also knows the mind of the Father in a way that is far above and beyond your natural understanding. Praying in the Spirit enables the Holy Spirit to assist you in achieving God's desired results.

A friend of mine was praying for a certain minister she had a burden for in prayer. Her prayer began something like this, "Father, I don't know how to pray for this man. I don't know anything else to pray. But because You continue to bring him before me, I submit myself to the intercession of Jesus for him."

Then after a short time of praying in the Spirit, this woman was aware that the Spirit of God was helping her pray. She began to weep with heart-rending groans, which were released in a language that she had never uttered before. She realized that she was experiencing another level of intercessory prayer.

After an interval of time, she began to pray in her native English. Listening, I heard her say; "Father, I thank You that this man is not ready to be offered up. His time of departure is not at hand. It is only after the fulfillment of all prophecies that he will say, 'I have fought a good fight; I have finished my course; I have kept the faith.' Then, Father, he will receive the crown of righteousness that You have laid up for him on that day."

We greatly rejoiced as we laughed, clapped our hands and danced about. Later I learned that Satan was trying to convince this minister that he was finished. The devil was harassing him with thoughts that no one wanted to hear what he had to say and that there was no longer a place for him in the body of Christ. We stood in the gap before God for this minister until he could see clearly Satan's assignment against him. Then he was able to stand and enforce the triumphant victory of Jesus Christ in his own life that God might be glorified.

It was the Holy Spirit who was searching out the minister's heart and who knew the plan of God for him. While the enemy was working against the minister with thoughts contrary to the will of God, the Spirit was praying that his faith would not fail and working on his behalf to open the eyes of his understanding.

As you become more intimately acquainted with God, He will use your availability as an instrument of prayer, releasing His will on the earth on behalf of others. Through the means of prayer, you can tear down strongholds as the Holy Spirit reveals truth that makes them free.

Praying in Travail

Travail is a term that is often misunderstood and shunned by some believers. The controversy includes two schools of thought: 1) Travail is not for today because Jesus travailed for us, and 2) No one will be born again until someone travails in prayer on his behalf. However, despite the controversy, the ministry of intercessory prayer continues both in heaven and in earth.

Travail is defined as "birth pangs" and is used symbolically in 1 Thessalonians 5:3 when referring to "the calamities which are to come upon men at the beginning of the Day of the Lord."[1]

Paul writes in Romans 8:19-26 that all of creation is in travail; mankind is in travail; and the Holy Spirit travails.

> **For [even the whole] creation (all nature) waits expectantly and longs earnestly for God's sons to be made known [waits for the revealing, the disclosing of their sonship].**
> **And not only the creation, but we ourselves too, who have and enjoy the firstfruits of the [Holy] Spirit [a foretaste of the blissful things to come] groan inwardly as we wait for the redemption of our bodies [from sensuality and the grave, which will reveal] our adoption (our manifestation as God's sons).**
> **Romans 8:19,23** AMP

Again in Paul's letter to the Galatians, he speaks of travail: **My little children, of whom I travail in birth again until Christ be formed in you** (Gal. 4:19). Here Paul seems to be questioning why he should have to travail in birth a second time for those who are born again. Does a mother have to experience travail a second time?

Paul is eager for these saints to arrive at maturity and produce spiritual children. He calls for them to walk as sons of God living in truth, no longer in bondage to Jewish laws or man's traditions. But we cannot ignore Paul's suggestion that he did travail before God on their behalf.

The Greek word translated *travail* is *odino*, a verb meaning "to experience the pains of parturition (literally or figuratively):—to travail in birth."[2]

The Old Testament prophet Isaiah foretold of the coming Messiah: **He shall see of the travail of his soul, and shall be satisfied** (Isa. 53:11). Jesus was the intercessor whom God required to suffer the birth pains of redemption for all mankind. A human intercessor could not be found, so God assumed the responsibility Himself in the person of His Son.

The legal side of redemption was provided for in the death and resurrection of God's Anointed. Today we are living on the vital side of redemption. But travail has not passed away. People will not be saved except when someone prays, decreeing the will of God for others' deliverance out of darkness and into the kingdom of God's Son.

Jesus continues His prayer ministry in heaven, interceding for the saints. The Holy Spirit deposits prayers in the hearts of a receptive people, and the prayers of Jesus are released into the earth through His body, just as spiritual endowments are released through the believers as the Spirit wills.

Therefore, as servants of Christ, our first priority in prayer is the salvation of mankind.

Travail originates in the heart of the Father, is released by Jesus and is then assigned to an available believer. With the aid of the Holy Spirit, the believer releases the heavenly prayers into the earth. The prayers ascend back to the throne of God, where He inhales the sweet-smelling incense. The essence of prayer is the very air that He breathes.

A Lesson Concerning Travail

How is travail released? The Holy Spirit so graphically illustrated this for me when I had the honor of witnessing the birth of a grandchild. Upon entering the delivery room, I was surprised at the calm, peaceful atmosphere. My daughter was dozing, and my son-in-law seemed very relaxed as he viewed a golf game on television. This was not my idea of a delivery room!

Since my daughter was sleeping, there wasn't much conversation. Nurses periodically entered the room quietly to check her vital signs. For a few short hours, nothing seemed to be happening. Even I began to doze; other times I went for short walks. The travail did not take place until the fullness of time—but it did take place!

When the time of travail arrived, the room was no longer calm. Nurses scurried in and out, slapping the door open, making urgent phone calls to hidden offices. My daughter was fully awake, her husband turned off the television and I backed into a corner, praying silently. It wasn't easy to watch my daughter in labor. I would have spared her that if I could have.

The nurses continued to dash in and out, and the urgency of the situation increased as my daughter's travail became more intense.

The nurse reporting to the doctor by phone was no longer asking for him but demanding that he come. My husband appeared in the midst of this situation but quickly retreated. Then the smiling doctor arrived and took his place. The final moments of birth were upon us.

Travail came without being worked up or instigated by moans and groans. A conception had occurred months before. Now out of a state of calmness, travail had begun, and it would not stop until the infant child gasped for her first breath and her wailing was heard.

By this time, I was standing by my daughter and her husband, so I saw her pain-filled, determined expression change to instant joy in a moment, in the twinkling of an eye. The love that flowed from this wife to her husband was then riveted on a premature, skinny, red-faced baby girl. This was the triumphant end of travail.

Later the Holy Spirit spoke to my spirit about this experience. He told me that this is what takes place in the womb of the human spirit when a child is delivered out of the authority of darkness and translated into the kingdom of light.

Conception occurs when the Holy Spirit, hovering over a willing vessel, deposits the spiritual seed in the womb of the spirit. In the fullness of time, travail comes upon the person and a spiritual birth occurs, thus ending travail. Groaning and moaning too deep to be uttered in articulate speech releases the travail from the person's spirit at the direction of the Holy Spirit.

This cry before the Father occurs in the secret place. There may be others present to assist, but all attention is given to the birth of those being born into the kingdom of God. When one is in travail in a prayer group, the others who are present can be likened to midwives in the birth room. They pray or quietly sing in the spirit, giving support to the birth process.

Travail emanates from the human spirit at the impulse of the Holy Spirit in the fullness of time; it cannot be worked up! Therefore, when you are in a public worship setting, exercise the self-control that has been given to you by God the Father.

We must learn to govern our human emotions and physical responses. The Holy Spirit is a gentleman. He does not overpower anyone against his or her will, nor does He work in a manner that calls undue attention to anyone.

God is due all the glory and the honor! **And we know that God causes everything to work together for the good of those who love God and are called according to his purpose for them** (Rom. 8:28 NLT).

The End of Travail

One night as a friend and I were praying together, she began to travail with a fervor that could not be expressed except in cries and moans. It appeared that she was in labor, and I prayed in my heavenly language.

As we continued to pray, the Holy Spirit revealed to us the identity of the couple for whom she was in travail. Even though we did not know the circumstances, we both recognized that it was a desperate situation. Their lives were in grave danger; it was a matter of life and death.

After an interval of time, the peace of God consumed us, and my prayer partner was released from travail. This peace that passes understanding ushered us into the rest of God. Deliverance had been brought forth and completed. It was the end of travail.

Later we learned that on that very day, the husband for whom we had been praying had acquired a pistol for the purpose of killing his wife and himself. When God found an available intercessor, the intercession of Jesus was released into the earth. Satan's plan was thwarted, and deliverance was birthed for two people who did not know how to go to God for themselves.

Ministry Begins in the Prayer Closet

Whatever is born of God has within it the seeds of victory. That is why it is so important to be certain that our ministries—whatever their capacity—are born of the will of God and not of the plans of man.

Individuals often ask me how to start a prayer ministry. First, make the commitment to obey God. Be willing to be a hidden part of the body of Christ. Study the Scriptures and fellowship with God. Tell Him you are available to pray for others.

Let's not allow the art of prayer to be lost or stolen from us through ignorance and neglect. Let us respond to the call of our Lord Jesus Christ to pray! As we maintain a teachable spirit and are quick to listen to wise counsel and advice, we will avoid many hurts along the way.

Now is the time to function on this planet as agents of the Lord Jesus Christ in intercession. But as we respond to the greater call, we must also continue to submit to transformation and personal spiritual growth. As representatives of Jesus Christ, we must dare to say, "Here am I, Lord. Use me as Your instrument of intercession in the earth today. Teach me to pray!"

So strip away the old nature, and **put on the new nature (the regenerate self) created in God's image, [Godlike] in true righteousness and holiness** (Eph.4:24 AMP). Be holy even as your heavenly Father is holy. Praise God that He called you to enter into partnership, praying prayers transported to you by the Holy Spirit from His heart to yours.

Talk with God, and listen to Him. Pray with all manner of prayer. As you do this, you will become a vessel God can use, an instrument He can choose to bring His will to pass on the earth.

CHAPTER 5

Purposes of Intercessory Prayer

The ultimate purpose of intercessory prayer is uncovered in the Lord's Prayer as recorded in Matthew 6:9 10: "Our Father in heaven, may Your Name be honored. May Your kingdom come soon. May Your will be done here on earth, just as it is in heaven."

Believers are colaborers with God. It is through the prayers of the saints that His will is established on the earth.

God's purposes far outreach the comprehension of the average churchgoer. Our sight is often so limited that we disregard His eternal purpose. We tend to become so caught up with the mundane affairs of life that we fail to see beyond today.

However, within the broad scope of God's plan, we can approach Him on behalf of others. We can pray as He has instructed us, that we may lead a quiet and peaceable life, influencing the lives of others for God. Thus, through prayer we are instrumental in establishing the intercession of Jesus on earth.

Spirit-Led Prayers Bring Deliverance

Each day Word Ministries receives mail from around the world. Most often, people are requesting prayer. At times, the volume is overwhelming.

One day as I sat in my den praying, I was overcome by the numerous prayer requests. The list of names seemed much too long, with too many names to mention.

As I contemplated how and where to begin, I prayed along these lines: "Father, I don't know where to begin. You know where prayer is most needed at this moment. I present my body as a living sacrifice, and I am willing to pray as You direct. Jesus, You are seated at the right hand of the Father, and I ask You, Holy Spirit, to reveal the intercession of Jesus to me. You know the plan of God for today."

If we are willing, the Holy Spirit comes alongside and helps us pray for others who need spiritual assistance. The Spirit knows the area under heaviest enemy attack. He knows the one whose heart is crying out for freedom.

As I prayed in the Spirit, I sensed that I was moving into that arena of prayer where the Holy Spirit takes hold together with us against our inability to produce results. I didn't know for whom I was praying, much less the desired results. But I sensed that I had hit upon a desperate situation. As I continued to pray, it wasn't long before the Lord revealed to me what that desperate situation was.

For many years, I had prayed for the deliverance and salvation of a particular young man. It was a joyous day when he shared with me how the presence of God entered his living room as he sat there all alone. His mother had given him *The Living Bible,* and he happened to open it to the book of Malachi. As he read, he realized his need for God and prayed a simple prayer. God delivered him, and since that time he had shared his testimony with many.

Some time later, much to my dismay, I learned that this young man had returned to his old lifestyle of drugs. I was furious. In my anger, I vowed I would no longer pray for him. God, however, has His ways of dealing with us.

As I prayed in the Spirit that morning in my den, I had a vision. In the vision, I saw myself standing before a building. It was obviously a business, and I recognized the location because I had been there before. When I walked around the building in the vision, I saw the young man for whom I had prayed. There he stood, engrossed in his work. He was totally unaware of three demonic spirits surrounding him. One demon had his fingers in the young man's ears; another had his hands over his eyes, and the third demon fastened his arms around the young man's head as though he were binding something.

With holy boldness, I spoke to the evil spirits. Upon hearing my voice, they became very agitated. I commanded them to go in the name of Jesus, and they left one by one. I continued to pray with my understanding as the Holy Spirit gave me utterance, ministering deliverance, peace and restoration to this young man. Then the vision ended.

I learned a valuable lesson from that experience: Submit to the will of God in everything, especially in how and for whom to pray.

A few days later, I had an opportunity to talk to this man for whom I had prayed. I casually asked him if God had visited him lately. He shared with me how he had yielded once again to smoking marijuana with his old buddies, believing he could walk in a middle of the-road type of consecration. He assumed he was in control and could afford an occasional smoke.

He continued to share with me: "I woke up the other morning and saw that I was no longer in the middle of the road—I was in the ditch! I had been confused about the voices I was hearing and was no longer sure about what was true. But this morning I heard God's voice, and I understood His message."

How grateful I was for the mercy of God and the direction of His Spirit! I could have missed it that day in prayer if I had allowed myself to follow *my thoughts* about praying for that man instead of following *God's heart* toward him.

So cooperate with the Holy Spirit in prayer and allow Him to lead you. You don't have to seek an "experience." Just submit to the leadership of the Holy Spirit. He knows the condition of every heart. He knows who is ready and able to receive.

Deliverance and restoration were accomplished in that man because the Holy Spirit searched the hearts of two individuals. He knew where my intercession was most needed that day. The result was that a prodigal son came home because God's will was established on the earth through prayer.

The Importance of Praying With a Pure Heart

Pleading the cause of others, as a lawyer does in a court of law, is another purpose of the prayer of intercession. (1 Tim. 2:1.) Again, in this type of prayer, Jesus is our example. Isaiah said of Him, **He bare the sin of many, and made intercession for the transgressors** (Isa. 53:12).

When praying for others, it is imperative to unite with the Holy Spirit. There is power in words, and if we don't pray according to the will of God, we will pray amiss, perhaps delaying the fulfillment of God's plan and purpose in an individual's life.

Ask the Holy Spirit to deposit the intercession of Jesus in your spirit, especially for those with whom you are emotionally involved. This is an area in which your own will and feelings can so easily come into play. And, if you aren't cautious, your own will and emotions can pull you contrary to the will of God in prayer.

When we react emotionally to a situation, allowing pride or indignation to control us, the picture becomes distorted and we may lose sense of the proper manner in which to pray. We may even find ourselves seeking revenge in certain situations.

Emotional prayers prayed with wrong motives can reinforce resistance against the will of God by the person for whom we pray. That's why it is imperative that we search our hearts before we attempt to plead the cause of another in prayer, especially if our own emotions are stirred about that person.

Prayer as a Defense or Vindication

It is impossible to pray for one's vindication while holding something against the person for whom you are praying. When you are praying, you must first forgive.

Unforgiveness is the principle hindrance to answered prayer. Jesus said,

And when ye stand praying, forgive, if ye have ought against any: that your Father also which is in heaven may forgive you your trespasses. But if ye do not forgive, neither will your Father which is in heaven forgive your trespasses.

Mark 11:25,26

If you are harboring unforgiveness in your heart, you cannot offer an acceptable prayer for that person. Furthermore, unforgiveness will become a stronghold in your mind. Pull it down with the weapons of your warfare, and let it go. Then once again you will be free to approach God with clean hands and a pure heart.

How often have we spent time in prayer that in the end proved fruitless because we walked in and out of our prayer closets with unacknowledged and unresolved issues in our own hearts and minds?

When you are "standing in the gap" before God, you are standing between a person and the judgment that has been pronounced upon sin, and it is important that you declare him forgiven. **"If you forgive someone's sins, they're gone for good. If you don't forgive sins, what are you going to do with them?"** (John 20:23 THE MESSAGE).

Holding their sins against those individuals for whom you are praying reinforces your wrong attitudes of judging and criticizing others—both of which are also hindrances to prayer.

For years I left this Scripture in the time frame when Jesus spoke these words, not wanting to misinterpret Jesus' meaning. But now I encourage parents of adult children to apply these two principles when praying for them:

1. Confess wrong attitudes you may have toward your child, and ask God's forgiveness.

3. Apply the blood of Jesus and forgive their sins (privately, in your prayer closet).

Now you are ready to stand between your child and the judgment God has pronounced on sins.

God isn't holding anything against the person you are praying for; therefore, you must not hold his sin against him. God is at work, drawing the person to Himself with cords and bands of love, so this is an opportunity for you to declare your authority to bind and loose as Jesus directed in Matthew 18:18.

Bind to the Will of God and
Loose From the Power of Sin

We are to *bind to* the mind, will and emotion of the person the Word of God, the truth of God, the blood of Jesus, the light of the gospel and the mind of Christ. We are to *loose from* the person spiritual blindness, wrong thinking and wrong attitudes in the name of Jesus.

Jesus gave us the keys to the kingdom, and He announced that **whatever you bind on earth will be bound in heaven, and whatever you loose on earth will be loosed in heaven** (Matthew 18:18 NKJV). This entire chapter is about interpersonal relationships.

In Liberty S. Savard's book, *Shattering Your Strongholds,* she explains how we can bind to ourselves and to others the will of God, the truth of God and the mind of Christ: We have the God-given power to loose from ourselves and others those strongholds that keep us divided.

For example, there was a time when I was having difficulty praying for Terri, one of our daughters. Terri had been saved at an early age; then later, in her teenage years, she was baptized with the Holy Spirit. Since the time of her salvation, she had faithfully read her Bible.

After graduating from college, Terri moved home, but her behavior was less than ideal in my estimation. We did not see eye to eye, and I found her views very disturbing. Our relationship was in transition, and I was very uncomfortable with it. This was a new season, and again, I found myself on my knees.

While my daughter was in high school, God had performed a miracle in our relationship. Before that, as a little girl, she had been my shadow and had "performed" her responsibilities in a manner that had pleased me.

This was the daughter who, when her mom and dad were having a communication problem that looked hopeless, had prayed: "Jesus is Mom and Dad's peace, who has made both one and has broken down the middle wall of partition between them. He has abolished in His flesh the enmity between them to make in Himself of the two, one new man, so making peace. He has reconciled both unto God in one body by the cross, having slain the enmity thereby." (Eph. 2:14-16.)

But now my daughter was suddenly very distant and isolated from the family. Home was just a place to eat, sleep and change clothes. But my duty, according to her, was to be at her beck and call.

It appeared that in her pursuit of others' approval, money and pleasure, our daughter had forsaken all we had taught her. God seemed to have very little space in her life. I began praying for her—apparently to no avail.

One day Everette said, "Germaine, you've grown very hard-hearted toward Terri. Have you considered forgiving her?"

Needless to say, my first reaction was self-defense, and I refused to accept his observation as true. But the Holy Spirit has many methods of leading us out of denial into reality. When I let go of my anger toward my husband, I realized he had spoken the truth.

Facing reality begins with a personal decision to walk in the Word. God's light exposed the darkness and I acknowledged my sin, repented and asked for forgiveness. God is faithful and just. He forgives and cleanses us from all unrighteousness. (1 John 1:9.)

As Terri grew more disobedient, I increased her restrictions, frustration set in and we experienced a communication breakdown. The Holy Spirit taught me to pray for her, and I wrote a prayer and prayed it until the breakthrough came.[1]

This prayer availed many rewards as my daughter and I experienced healing and restoration to a spiritual tone of mind and heart.

Not only did my daughter's attitudes change, but God also taught me more about working out my own salvation. As a result, God exposed strongholds in my life that had to come down. Destroying strongholds is imperative in achieving spiritual growth and emotional wholeness. Her will and mine were bound to the will of God, and we were loosed from the strongholds that divided us.

Intercession in Accordance With God's Will

Our prayers must be in accordance with God's purpose and plan. For example, many times the tribe of Judah committed the sin of idolatry. On one occasion, God told Jeremiah he was not to pray for Judah, nor was he to lift up a cry for them or make intercession for them. (Jer. 7:16.) Later Jeremiah did intercede on their behalf, but his prayer was never answered.

In 1 John 5:16, John writes,

If you see any Christian sinning in a way that does not lead to death, you should pray, and God will give that person life. But there is a sin that leads to death, and I am not saying you should pray for those who commit it.

We must know the voice of the Holy Spirit and allow Him to lead us in our praying. We can't just get upset with people and decide we will withhold intercessory prayer from them because we want to see them punished.

Romans 12:17-19 gives us guidelines to follow in prayer along this line. We are never to seek vengeance in prayer or attempt to pay back evil for evil to anyone. Romans 12:19 (NLT) says, **Dear friends, never avenge yourselves. Leave that to God.**

Intercessors are to pray and live in such a way that is honorable before both God and man. They are to do their part to live in peace with everyone as much as possible. The joyous intercessor is always ready to release the mercy cry: **Father, forgive them; they know not what they do** (Luke 23:34).

When we pray erroneously, our own words will come back to judge us. Therefore, we must approach God with clean hands and pure hearts; otherwise, He will look for another who is willing to pray His will.

Commending Others to God

When we pray for our loved ones and others, we can commend them to God according to Hebrews 7:25 and Romans 8:26-28 for salvation, healing, reconciliation and restoration. In the prayer closet, hidden away with God, we depend on the Holy Spirit to reveal the kinds of prayer necessary to establish the eternal plan of God on the earth for them. In doing so, we positively affect individuals, communities and nations to the glory of God.

Intercession and God's Eternal Plan

God's overall plan includes the restoration of all things, the manifestation of the sons of God and the fulfillment of His promises to Israel. (Rom. 8-11.) The Age of Grace—which is also known as the Age of the Gentiles—is approaching completion. Soon the Rapture (which is the catching away of the saints described in 1 Thessalonians 4) will take place.

At this time, we shall see Jesus as He is. A period of seven years of tribulation will follow, to be consummated at the Second Advent of Jesus Christ when He returns to earth with His saints. He will then establish the kingdom of heaven on earth for a thousand-year millennial reign, and **the government shall be upon his shoulder** (Isaiah 9:6). Israel as a nation will recognize the Messiah. Jerusalem will be the capital city of his reign, and God's promises to Israel will be fulfilled. (Isa. 2:3.)

The saints will reign with Him, and Israel will be priests of the Lord to all other nations. And when all things are subdued unto Him, then shall the

Son also Himself be subject unto the Father who placed all things under Him, that God may be all in all. (1 Cor. 15:28.) Thus shall be the consummation of the everlasting plan of God's redemption of man.

Preparing the Way
for the Consummation of the Ages

You see, God's purposes are eternal. And the prayers of the saints are preparing the way of the Lord as He sets the stage for the millennial reign of Christ.

> **O the depth of the riches both of the wisdom and knowledge of God! how unsearchable are his judgments, and his ways past finding out!**
>
> **For who hath known the mind of the Lord? Or who hath been his counsellor? Or who hath first given to him, and it shall be recompensed unto him again? For of him, and through him, and to him, are all things: to whom be glory for ever. Amen.**
>
> **Romans 11:33-36**

The poetry of the *King James Version* translation thrills the heart. These very words arouse an intense desire to continue walking by faith, cooperating with God's plan and praying always without fainting or turning cowardly.

We are to pray for one another for several reasons: We are all one body. We have the same Spirit. We have all been called to the same glorious future.

> **We are all one body, we have the same Spirit, and we have all been called to the same glorious future. There is only one Lord, one faith, one baptism, and there is only one God and Father, who is over us all and in us all and living through us all.**
>
> **Ephesians 4:4-6 NLT**

Therefore, because we are members one with another, each joint can supply strength to the other through prayer.

Satan's tactics are designed to keep the body of Christ divided, and he uses our unresolved issues to separate us. That's why Paul admonished us to keep ourselves united in the Holy Spirit and to bind ourselves together with peace. We are to work together as partners who belong to God, standing together against the devices of the enemy.

Put on God's armor so that you can successfully resist all the devil's craftiness.

> **For our fight is not against any physical enemy: it is against organizations and powers that are spiritual. We are up against the unseen power that controls this dark world, and spiritual agents from the very headquarters of evil.**
>
> Ephesians 6:12 PHILLIPS

The Old Testament way for dealing with those who opposed God was to execute vengeance and wrath upon them. Under the Old Covenant, King David considered the enemies of God to be his own personal enemies, and he physically annihilated as many of them as possible. But the New Testament saint administers his God-given authority in the spiritual realm, not the physical realm, staying ever alert to the enemy's devices to keep the body of Christ divided and defeated.

So do not approach God with accusations against your brothers and sisters; they are not your enemies. To pray against any other human being—even those who despitefully use you—is to misuse the power of prayer.

As we take our place in prayer in these last days, we will all at one time or another be faced with impossible situations that we must pray through. Jack Hayford, pastor of The Church on the Way in Van Neys, California, defines prayer as the act of invading the impossible. In his book, *Prayer Is Invading the Impossible*, he writes: "There is a way to face impossibility. Invade it! Not with a glib speech of high hopes. Not in anger. Not with resignation. Not through stoical self-control. But with violence. And prayer provides the vehicle for this kind of violence."[2]

How do we invade an impossible situation with a godly "violence" that subdues the enemy? The psalmist David aptly described praise as the kind of "violent" or aggressive invasion that transforms the impossible into the possible by bringing the power of God on the scene.

In Psalm 18:32-39 (NLT), David spoke of God's help in waging physical battle against the Lord's enemies.

> **God arms me with strength; he has made my way safe. He makes me as surefooted as a deer, leading me safely along the mountain heights. He prepares me for battle; he strengthens me to draw a bow of bronze. You have given me the shield of your salvation. Your right hand supports me; your gentleness has made me great. You have made a wide path for my feet to keep them from slipping. I chased my enemies and caught them; I did not stop until they were conquered. I struck them down so they could not get up; they fell beneath my feet. You have armed me with strength for the battle; you have subdued my enemies under my feet.**

Under the new covenant, we also experience God's grace to help in time of need as we exercise our authority against the enemy in prayer. We are the enforcers of the victory won at Calvary.

So let the high praises of God be in your mouth and a two-edged sword in your hand to execute vengeance not on people, but on the satanic kingdom. Use prayer as a spiritual weapon on behalf of those held in bondage by the powers of darkness. Do your part to prepare the way for the consummation of God's eternal plan in these last days!

CHAPTER 6

Wisdom in Prayer

P rayer is not dictating to God; it is a conversation with the awesome, majestic Creator of the universe. Prayer is a joint spiritual activity with the Holy Spirit, who is the Spirit of wisdom and understanding. Prayers that produce results are prayed according to knowledge and offered in agreement with the wisdom of God.

The Holy Spirit is an intercessor who cannot fail because He is the Spirit of counsel and of power, the Spirit of knowledge and the fear of the Lord. (Isa. 11:2.) One facet of the present-day ministry of the Holy Spirit is to help us when we don't know how, what or for whom to pray.

Deuteronomy 6:4-5 (NIV) tells us what is required in order for us to obtain and walk in God's wisdom: **Hear, O Israel: The Lord our God, the Lord is one. Love the Lord your God with all your heart and with all your soul and with all your strength.**

We cannot love, honor and revere One whom we do not know. In the garden of prayer, we become more intimately acquainted with the author and finisher of our faith. Prayer is a key to unlocking the door of our innermost being, which is where we receive wisdom.

In our private devotions, we pay homage to our God, and publicly we worship Him with our lifestyle—our conversation and behavior. We also offer up sacrifices of praise in verbal adoration. This worship of our King of kings and Lord of lords is personal, for, as Proverbs 1:7 (NIV) says, **The fear of the Lord is the beginning of knowledge.**

Maintaining Unity in the Body

Wisdom prays, "Your will be done on earth as it is in heaven." Yet too often we give place to the devil, who seeks to counterfeit and frustrate the grace of God. When we hear from God, we are assured that He will confirm His will. Our thinking is finite; His is infinite.

Satan's favorite tactic is to divide and conquer. People in the body of Christ fight over speaking in tongues, spiritual warfare, travail, intercessory prayer, the issue of "once saved always saved"—and the list goes on and on. Believers build mental "strongholds" to protect their beliefs, becoming adamant in what they perceive as truth.

Paul exhorted believers to be wary of this destructive tactic of the enemy. Paul wrote,

> **I hope all of you who are mature Christians will agree on these things. If you disagree on some point, I believe God will make it plain to you. But we must be sure to obey the truth we have learned already.**
>
> **Philippians 3:15,16 NLT**

What things can we agree on? To answer this, let's go back to the beginning of Paul's letter, the point at which he gives thanks to God for his brothers and sisters in the Lord.

I have learned from those with whom I disagree and from those with whom I agree. We are to pray one for each other and make our requests with a heart full of joy because we are partners in spreading the good news about Christ. And we are to follow Paul's theme of love, joy, partnership and overflowing love for one another. We are mutually dependent on one another; therefore, we should agree wholeheartedly with each other on the basic truths that really matter.

We are to pray, binding to others and ourselves the knowledge of Christ so we all may experience the mighty power that raised Him from the dead.

Prayer is a vital pillar in any church or spiritual endeavor. Without prayer, a church becomes a social organization, failing to meet the spiritual needs of the congregation. Even though the Word of God may be taught, without prayer it becomes a legalistic form, void of power. Prayer is essential! That's why one of Satan's primary plots is to eliminate effective prayer, as well as all other spiritual weapons, from the body of Christ.

Your Place of Prayer
in the Local Church

Everyone is to pray. However, there are many who sense "the call" to intercede on behalf of their pastor and the leadership of their church. This prayer assignment is of utmost importance. Those who respond to this call must be obedient to the leadership, who is responsible for teaching them the art of intercessory prayer.

It is my belief that every member of the body of Christ has a special place. No member is called to just sit on the pew. So ask God to reveal His designated place for you in your local church.

When I considered working in one of the various departments of the church, I wanted to serve where I could support the vision of our pastor. When I asked God to reveal His assignment to me, He said, "I have called you here to intercede for the associate pastor." This man I was assigned to pray for is now the senior pastor of our church.

The responsibility of leadership is to equip God's people to do His work and build up the church, the body of Christ. Intercessors are the "Hurs" and "Aarons" supporting the leadership. We are to obey the spiritual leaders and do what they say, praying in agreement with their vision. We follow them as they follow Jesus.

Teach Us To Pray

In the beginning stages of my prayer life, I met with a group in my church. We sat in a circle and prayed sentence prayers. It was difficult for me to listen to the others because I was searching for something intelligent to pray when it was my turn. But week after week that I attended, I learned and became more confident. Eventually, this group disbanded, and I was left to search for another group.

A little knowledge can sometimes give us a false sense of security. In my new-found courage, I sometimes walked where angels fear to tread!

My next experience with group prayer was in a small home group, and I was the facilitator. My first prayer partner also met with us.

My lack of knowledge opened the door for familiar spirits. I had more zeal than wisdom—but God was rich in mercy!

My heart was fixed on God, and I wanted to learn to pray with a group of people who were dedicated to pray for others.

I am so thankful for God's faithfulness and patience. Had we never started, I don't know when we would have learned. We submitted ourselves to the leadership of the Holy Spirit, but it would take time for Him to teach us the difference between the "discerning of spirits" and the work of familiar spirits.

As we prayed for an individual, it seemed that his weaknesses, faults and shortcomings were made known to us. We called every symptom a demon. We spent hours reviewing and rehearsing the secrets that were being revealed. And when a group member who knew the person in need of prayer confirmed our revelation, we just knew that we were hearing from God.

We searched the Bible for Scriptures we could use to drive away the demons. But, in fact, we sometimes reinforced an individual's resistance to receiving truth. In spite of our mistakes, we saw many answers to prayer and continued our pursuit of praying prayers that avail much.

The person who does nothing learns nothing. In our quest to learn how to pray, my prayer group made mistakes. But prayer is an on-the-job learning experience. Our responsibility as believers is to remain flexible in the potter's hands as He molds us and makes us into useful instruments of prayer. God is faithful to provide a "laboratory"—a safe place—for us where we can learn, grow and achieve the knowledge that is sorely needed for praying effectively.

An intercessory prayer group is one bandwagon that the most naïve believer can join. But in some circles, intercessors are set apart and given inappropriate significance that they are not able to handle. These same people are often looked upon as being spiritually mature; yet many times they have not worked through their own particular personal issues.

They fell in love with the lover of their souls, Jesus, and they desire to walk in newness of life, but they are still unfamiliar with the elementary teachings of the Scriptures. They need someone to teach them. Yet others, who feel unworthy to approach God, may view them as strong people who "have it all together."

God has given gifts to the church—apostles, prophets, evangelists, pastors and teachers—to equip the body of Christ for the work of the ministry. Every new believer joining an intercessory prayer group needs someone to disciple him in the ways of God and teach him to pray. Otherwise, his zeal will overreach his wisdom, and his efforts will be thwarted through a lack of knowledge, delaying spiritual growth and often causing unnecessary emotional pain.

A common fault among those of us who intercede is judging those for whom we are praying. Its companion is a critical spirit. We who have grown up in judgmental, critical homes and church environments may mistakenly view "judging others" as the exercise of "spiritual insight."

God enables us to "face ourselves" as we grow in His grace and wisdom. Here's what I do: After binding my mind, will and emotions to the wisdom of God, the grace of God and the mind of Christ, I loose a judgmental and critical attitude and its effects from my mind. It takes time to change old thought patterns and put on the new man created in Christ Jesus. By the grace of God, we adopt new mental and spiritual attitudes. We study and meditate on wisdom that is from above, learning its attributes. We sow in peace, raising a harvest of righteousness.

In retrospect, I see that the chief personal issue that had a communal effect on this first prayer group was a tendency to judge others. We had a keen sense of justice, but then God taught us mercy. The miraculous wonder of God is that His grace is greater than our weaknesses.

Other redemptive aspects of this group were honest hearts and a deep longing to know the fundamentals of prayer. Also, our fervent prayer was that all unfavorable information would be removed from our minds so we would never reveal secrets outside our closed doors. It was our sincere desire to see those for whom we were praying delivered and set free from bondage.

The Holy Spirit began to show us the truths of John 17, in which Jesus interceded for us. Also, the Spirit of God revealed the prayers of Paul to us, and we began to use these as models for prayer.

I marveled that Paul prayed for the churches, not because of their individual weaknesses, but because they were chosen and adopted by God. The blood of Jesus Christ had remitted their sins. He identified them according to the will and purpose of God.

Enter God's 'Classroom'
and Learn To Pray

You, too, have a Helper who cannot fail. So determine to be controlled by the Holy Spirit. Listen to the inner witness as you study the Word of God.

You will learn to trust the leading of the Holy Spirit as He guides you into all reality. He will take the ways of Jesus and reveal them to you, showing you things to come. (John 16:13,14.)

Praying the Word of God releases the anointing of God. So dare to believe. Pray all manner of prayer—both with your understanding and in the Spirit. Apply the prayer of binding and loosing that destroys strongholds, reasonings and high, lofty thoughts that exalt themselves above the knowledge of God. The anointing goes beyond *breaking* yokes—it destroys, crushes to powder and utterly annihilates every yoke of bondage.

If you are praying with a prayer group, begin the session with praise and worship. Praise is an effective prayer weapon. It stops the avenger and stills his raging taunts. When your prayers begin to lag, it is time to praise the Lord.

Bind the mind, will and emotions of the group members to the plan of God for that particular session. Then loose wrong attitudes and unnecessary talking from them. You see, valuable time can be wasted on information that the Holy Spirit would never reveal about a person. We are not ignorant of the enemy's devices, and we can learn to avoid pitfalls designed to hinder our prayers.

Hindrances to Prayer:
Lack of Knowledge

In the early days, I prayed with great enthusiasm and extravagant zeal. Sensing an urgency to pray, I "felt" the power to make choices that could change my destiny and the destiny of others. Believing that I possessed revelation knowledge in spite of my lack of education in God's Word gave me a feeling of great satisfaction.

I was studying and growing in the knowledge of the Word, but my zeal in many instances exceeded the correct and vital knowledge I needed for praying effectively. Paul talked about this kind of zeal in Romans 10:2 (AMP):

> **I bear them witness that they have a [certain] zeal and enthusiasm for God, but it is not enlightened and according to [correct and vital] knowledge.**

Zeal reinforces our motivation to pray. But along with our zeal, may we be

> **...filled with the full (deep and clear) knowledge of His will in all spiritual wisdom [in comprehensive insight into the ways and purposes of God] and in understanding and discernment of spiritual things.**
>
> **Colossians 1:9** AMP

Zeal according to knowledge is not based on our emotions.

As we grow in the grace and knowledge of Jesus Christ, we become aware of and learn to avoid the designs of the devil.

Down through the centuries, Satan has experienced the power of prayer and its results. That's why his purpose is to discourage and deter believers from pursuing the challenge of persistent prayer. For instance, Satan has duped some into believing that if they respond to the call to pray for others, they will suffer greater buffeting.

Don't buy this lie. The Scriptures don't teach this. Jesus said we would all have trials and tribulations; they come whether we pray or not. But praying for others doesn't increase our chances for the enemy's attacks unless we open the door for them. Let us not give Satan any more power than he has. And he has no power over the believer who is walking in his or her authority in Christ!

Zeal is necessary in maintaining an effective prayer life, but you will not always experience feelings of enthusiasm. In fact, there will be times when you really don't want to pray; you will have other things you would rather do.

We receive many calls at our ministry from people who ask, "What can I do to recapture the zeal to pray?" We tell them to first recognize that prayerlessness is a sin and repent.

Repentance calls for a change in thinking. Ask the Holy Spirit to expose any wrong thought patterns or attitudes you may be harboring and to renew your mind by the Word of God. God will transform you into a new person by helping you change the way you think. Your faith cannot be exercised apart from prayer. Prayer is the doorway to knowing God.

Prayerlessness is a product of the carnal mind. That's why Galatians 5:25 says, **If we live in the Spirit, let us also walk in the Spirit.**

Resist the temptation to neglect your prayer and study time with God. Submit to God by obeying His Word. Pray without ceasing. Study to show yourself approved unto God, rightly dividing the Word of Truth. This is an opportunity to become more intimately acquainted with the Father.

As you may have already discovered, attempting to overcome prayer-lessness by human strength and striving only results in more condemnation. Andrew Murray addresses a diminished zeal for prayer in his book, *The Prayer Life*. He shares an illustration of a woman who went to her minister for advice.

The minister instructed her:

> As you go to your inner chamber, however cold and dark your heart may be, do not try in your own might to force yourself into the right attitude. Bow before Him, and tell Him that He sees what a sad state you are in and that your only hope is in Him. Trust Him with a childlike trust to have mercy upon you, and wait upon Him. In such a trust you are in a right relationship to Him. You have nothing—He has everything.[1]

God always meets us where we are. Our God is always present—He is always there.

The Measuring Stick

In my early days of searching out the truth for the purpose of praying prayers that avail much, I attended several different prayer groups.

If you will look to the inner witness and the Word of God for confirmation, such experiences can be rewarding. Otherwise, it is possible to fall into great confusion as you encounter the many methods, teachings and voices that are out there to program your thinking.

What can we use to confirm what is truth? God has provided us with an accurate measuring stick of truth—the Word of God. So ask yourself, *Does the Word of God support what is taking place here?*

At one prayer meeting, a young lady who was obviously a new Christian wanted the group to pray that a certain mountain of difficulty in her life be removed and cast into the sea according to Mark 11:23. She went on to reveal that the "mountain" was her husband. So everyone began to dutifully and earnestly pray that the young woman's mountain be removed and cast into the sea. Much zeal went into that prayer, but the prayer was in error. Thank God for His longsuffering and His protection!

From the account this young woman gave, I ascertained that the problem revolved around her attending prayer meetings, church services, Bible studies and seminars while her husband sat home alone. This had become a nightly occurrence.

On this particular night, the husband had asked his wife to stay home with him. As the woman recounted the event, her voice rose to new levels of intensity. She said, "I knew this was the devil wanting me to stay home. So I stomped my foot and said with boldness, 'I know who you are—you're the devil! Satan, get thee behind me!'"

This might be an amusing account, but it happens much too often. And then wives wonder why their husbands are so stubborn about God!

Advice to Prayer Group Leaders

Prayer group leaders have to exercise much wisdom in directing others in the principles and practices of prayer. This requires Bible study and spending time alone with God.

As leaders, we must allow the Word of God to divide between the soul and spirit, let go of our personal opinions and avoid taking on the offenses of another. Only then will we be able to rightly divide the Word of Truth.

Many different personalities congregate in the name of prayer. For instance, I have seen prayer group members release unacknowledged personal emotions inappropriately while praying for requests that are similar in nature to unresolved issues in their own lives. Judgment is pronounced with great wrath and indignation because of the emotion of the person praying, not by the direction of the Holy Spirit.

A prayer group leader is responsible to address such issues with much love and boldness. When intercessors are sensitive to the needs of their own group members, personal healing will flow to them even while they pray for others.

Our responsibilities as prayer group leaders are often overwhelming, and our communication skills are often stretched beyond human knowledge. But we must remember that we are not sufficient unto ourselves—*God alone* is our sufficiency.

Often the Holy Spirit gives special abilities in the form of a word of knowledge or a word of wisdom. Be available to Him; then depend on Him to give these abilities as needed.

Don't be afraid to establish guidelines for regular group members. Make it a prerequisite that everyone is first of all a student of the Word of God.

It has been my experience that those who are called by God to a particular group have similar interests and they respect the leader who relies on the written Word for guidance. In a church or organized ministry environment, the leader must be in submission to the pastor and church doctrines. The leader is to be an example of godly wisdom and submission to authority through precept and practice.

Prayer is serious business. It can either be a vital asset to a church or a detriment to the spiritual condition and reputation of that ministry. Therefore, a prayer group setting is not the appropriate place for group members to air their grievances against their pastor, spouse or other group members.

If you have been offended by someone, go privately to the one who has offended you and express your feelings, requesting clarification. Then listen and seek to understand without interruption. Be quick to listen and slow to speak.

Given the importance of these principles to the welfare of the local church, it is of utmost importance that Christian leaders adhere to Paul's admonition in 1 Thessalonians 5:12 (AMP) before placing someone in a position of authority or church leadership: **Get to know those who labor among you [recognize them for what they are].**

Misuse of Scriptures

In our prayer groups, we can sometimes get in the way of what God wants to do. Many times we misunderstand the prayer of agreement Jesus presented in Matthew 18:19:

> **Again I say unto you, That if two of you shall agree on earth as touching any thing that they shall ask, it shall be done for them of my Father which is in heaven.**

The Lord taught me much about the principles and practice of this form of prayer after a vivid experience in my marriage. The ladies in the prayer group that I had organized "agreed" with me that Everette, my husband, would go with me to an upcoming seminar where one of my favorite faith teachers would be speaking.

At this time, Everette didn't seem interested in the work God had called me to do. He also didn't share my enthusiasm for attending church or spiritual seminars. He was gracious and never hindered me from going, but he refused to attend.

A desire to have Everette accompany me to gatherings became a consuming fire within me. I tried every ploy to coerce him into going with me. I heard testimonies of how God was bringing couples into total harmony and agreement. I even saw it happening in the marriages of some of the ladies who were attending the Bible study I was teaching.

Prominent speakers were teaching that if one marriage partner was called to a ministry, both were called. My husband disagreed with this belief. I felt that I was being judged and found wanting by those who walked together in the ministry as one.

Before opening day of an important three-day seminar, I played the game my husband and I always played when I wanted him to do something special for me. I would try to diminish its importance and never position myself for a yes or no answer. Our history together taught me to expect a no when I asked him for a favor. Sometimes the no meant "Absolutely no way!" Other times it meant maybe. Once in a while, Everette would accommodate me.

Each time I talked about the upcoming meeting, Everette never said he wouldn't go. So I assumed that this was one of those times he would do what I wanted.

My excitement escalated when the idea came to ask for the prayer group's agreement. We did some powerful praying, declaring again and again that Everette would be transformed at these meetings.

There was no doubt in my mind that Everette would go. This would be a wonderful opportunity for the ladies to see the power of prayer at work. After all, I believed and I did not doubt in my heart; therefore, God would be glorified.

The first night of the meeting came and went—but Everette did not. The second night came and went. Everette stayed home. Finally, it was the third and closing night of the seminar—God's last chance to answer our "binding" prayer of agreement.

Two seats were reserved in the front row of the auditorium: one for me and one for my husband. As the time for departure drew near, I grew more excited because I know that God always comes through.

Looking at the clock one more time, I realized that it was getting late. Feelings of anxiety began to arise. *This is simply a test of my faith,* I thought. Fighting back my emotions, I walked into the room where Everette was sitting, only to hear him say, "If you are going to the service tonight, you need to leave."

Struggling to open my mouth to explain why this was so important to me, he closed the subject. "You and your friends cannot and will not 'confess' me into going downtown to that meeting. I am staying home to watch the World Series."

An usher met me at the entrance and walked me down that *long* aisle to the reserved seats. I could feel everyone's eyes following each step. Hoping that my smile was in place, I avoided looking at anyone directly.

My inner turmoil was raging. I knew that God could not fail, so I knew that I had misunderstood something, and even worse, I had misguided others.

Self-pity kept nudging my thoughts. *How dare Everette allow me to drive into downtown Atlanta by myself! I don't know of any other husband who wants his wife to go downtown alone—much less at night!*

My friends and I had done everything we knew to do, and we truly believed we'd get our answer! Besides, I had put "corresponding action" to my faith by refusing all rides to the meeting on this final evening. I had acted in accordance with my faith, and that was supposed to be the measure of what I received. (Matt. 9:29.) We'd had no lack of zeal—but still, there was no Everette at my side any of the three nights.

You may make mistakes due to immature zeal. However, when you are looking for answers, God will move heaven and earth if necessary to get His truth to you—the truth that makes you free. In this situation, the group members didn't lose faith, and I expected God to reveal to me where I had missed Him.

The word *manipulation* kept coming to my mind—a word I was increasingly sure was God's answer to my question, "Where did I go wrong?" But it would take time and study to understand how this "prayer of agreement" was manipulation. Assuming responsibility for my mistake was very painful, and I didn't want to believe that I could have participated in anything outside of God's will.

As I sought God for answers, the Holy Spirit led me to Galatians 5:19-20 in the *King James Version*, verses which speak of the works of the flesh. Much to my chagrin, I realized that in attempting to conform the will of another person to my own I had practiced a form of witchcraft—a work of the flesh.

God is faithful. He forgives and He exposes strongholds, revealing wrong thinking and wrong attitudes. We are to strip ourselves of the old former nature; then we are to put on the new man created in Christ Jesus and walk in victory. The blood of Jesus cleanses us from all unrighteousness.

As a nice Southern lady, I had mastered the techniques of manipulation—a stronghold exposed by the Spirit of God. Fear of rejection prevented me from being straightforward concerning my personal needs and desires. James 3:17 tells us that wisdom from above is straightforward, but I found it difficult to place myself in a position where I might be told no outright.

Without realizing it, I had attempted to control another person's decision through the power of prayer and positive confession. I had not trusted God to direct Everette, and I didn't trust Everette to obey God.

So often we determine what we want and then expect God to answer our prayer in spite of His will. It seems that it is possible to find a Scripture to support almost anything we want God to do. But are we rightly dividing the Word of Truth?

Not only had I not walked in wisdom in that situation, but I also had not walked in love. Remember, one of the characteristics of love is that it doesn't insist on its own way.

Again and again I have found that when our prayers are not being answered, it can be traced back to walking outside of the love of God.

It was not my friends' agreement that I needed in that situation—it was Everette's! Knowing that God had forgiven me and cleansed me, I asked my husband's forgiveness and released him to make his own choices without my interference.

He had always given me the freedom to make my own decisions. Now I returned to him what he had given me—the freedom to hear from God and to obey the voice of the Good Shepherd as an individual.

The very next year, there was another seminar scheduled. To my surprise, Everette not only attended voluntarily, but he also served as an usher by his own volition. I went with him to all the evening services!

Objectivity: The Key To Praying for Loved Ones

It is sometimes difficult for people to pray for their spouses objectively. Over the years, many women have come to our ministry wanting to know how to pray for their husbands. In my personal ministry to them, I have uncovered certain common issues.

We are sincere women who love God and want to do His will. We desire to express the newfound love we are experiencing without rebuke. At the same time, we are seeking certain basic fulfillments—to be loved, to feel significant and to feel secure. We are looking for and need emotional connection with our spouses. In other words, we need emotional support and our spouse's assurance that we are acceptable and worthy as individuals.

As a result of persistent and useless maneuvers designed to turn our households into the paths of righteousness, we arrive at our wit's end. In this condition, we gladly assume the belief that through the power of prayer we can change our spouses!

We relentlessly set out to bring about change, experiencing spiritual authority for the first time. We believe that praying accurately will positively transform our circumstances.

But alas! Much too often, we forget that prayer is to be done in secret and that the weapons of our warfare are not carnal. We discuss, we argue, we debate, we deliberate, we storm—and then we hide out so we can think about how to redefine and regroup for another round.

Grappling with flesh and blood, we try to help God accomplish our prayers. Meanwhile, the Holy Spirit is always present to lead us into all truth, revealing strongholds that have protected our wrong thought patterns, ideas and beliefs.

Peter wrote that the husband might be won by the godly behavior of the wife without discussion. (1 Peter 3:1,2.) But it takes time to put off ungodly habits, establish new patterns in our relationships and renew our minds to the Word of God.

Before circumstances change, we find that God is seeking to bring about changes in our own thought patterns and attitudes. Change always produces change, but seldom does it come in the manner we expect it, and it may not always be the change we would choose. Are we willing to change at any personal cost?

Wanting to walk in love, we listen to inaccurate teaching on submission that reinforces our belief that we are not to have needs or wants. We develop a "savior complex" and blame ourselves when our spouses are not walking with God. Unfounded shame and guilt keep us in bondage to a past over which we have no control. We doubt our ability to assume responsibility for ourselves and feel that our wants and needs are not important.

Some teachers even instruct women to look to their unsaved husbands for spiritual guidance rather than trust their own ability to listen to the still, small voice within. (1 Kings 19:12.)

The majority of women who come to us want to know and understand truth. They believe that the truth will heal unspoken hurts, displace unacknowledged anger and set them free from unresolved issues in their lives and marriages. Having looked to another human being to complete them, they are emotionally entangled.

When we are willing to look at ourselves honestly and assume responsibility for our own behavior, healing comes. Then we are able to pray objectively for our families.

Objectivity is an asset when praying for others. It enables us to make a deliberate move from demanding our own way to praying according to the will of God so that He might be glorified.

Ask the Holy Spirit to reveal Scripture that will empower you to pray according to His will and purpose for your spouse. Praying for your marriage partner will also bring healing and restoration to you. Your prayers will often place demands on you to change your beliefs and ideas about what a marriage should be. This same principle applies when praying for your children or other family members.

Much more often than I care to admit, my own needs and desires clouded my prayers for Everette. I realize now that my prayers for him were prayers of petition—not prayers of intercession. The petitions were based on wanting my will to be done.

As I grew in the grace and the knowledge of my Lord and Savior Jesus Christ, my prayers changed. God would not allow me to take away Everette's power of choice, and I began to pray for the will of God to be done on earth in Everette as it is in heaven. My petitions gave way to intercession. "Not my will, Father, but Yours be done" became my melody of prayer.

Pray for your mate according to God's Word, not according to your personal desires that have not yet conformed to the will of God. Expect the grace of God to enable you to accept your spouse just as God in Christ Jesus accepted you.

Bind your mind, will and emotions to the will of God and the mind of Christ that you may pray the intercession of Jesus. He is praying for you and your spouse. Loose yourself and your mate from wrong beliefs and mind-sets. Whether you have judged your spouse's behavior accurately or inaccurately, your judgment will control your prayer attitude.

The Holy Spirit began to direct my prayers for Everette, and He gave me many Scriptures in support of these prayers. (See the prayers "Husbands" in *Prayers That Avail Much, Volume 1*[2] and "The New Creation Marriage" in *Prayers That Avail Much, Volume 2.*[3])

When I saw the error of my ways, I ran to God, asking Him to forgive me for misusing Scripture and for trying to play the Holy Spirit through human efforts of manipulation and control.

Your spouse is not your enemy. Your warfare is in the realm of the spirit. Ephesians 6:12 says,

> **For we wrestle not against flesh and blood, but against principalities, against powers, against the rulers of the darkness of this world, against spiritual wickedness in high places.**

These forces of darkness are constantly attempting to influence your thoughts.

Thank God, His Word says,

> **Every Scripture is God-breathed (given by His inspiration) and profitable for instruction, for reproof and conviction of sin, for correction of error and discipline in obedience, [and] for training in righteousness (in holy living, in conformity to God's will in thought, purpose, and action).**
>
> **2 Timothy 3:16** AMP

So when you make a mistake in prayer, repent. Ask for forgiveness and then renew your mind to the Word of God. Cast down strongholds of doubt and suspicion. Thank God for another opportunity for learning, growing and achieving.

Emotion vs. Spirit

For some reason, we tend to think that the greater the emotional display in our prayer groups, the greater the anointing. The louder the crying and the more boisterous the praying, the more effective the prayers. Unfortunately, in certain assemblies, emotions become the measuring rod for a move of the Spirit.

In every prayer group, there is usually at least one member who is more emotional than the others. Group members tend to look upon this person as being highly anointed and very spiritual. Before they realize it, they begin to depend on the emotional reactions of this individual as a sign of the significance of their prayers or as evidence to determine whether or not the prayer has been answered.

For example, as long as this person is crying, the rest of the group continues to pray fervently. Laughter is a sign that the prayer has been heard and answered, so at that point the group moves on to another prayer subject.

But we can and should learn to separate emotion from faith as we pray. A member of our group learned this as she prayed for a friend. The group member thought that her praying was in vain. Her feelings remained numb no matter how hard she tried to work up a good cry. But that very afternoon, she received a phone call that confirmed God had heard and answered prayer.

The Holy Spirit helps us when we don't know how to pray or what to pray for. We learn to walk by faith and not by feelings.

Even though emotions are God-given, nowhere does He tell us that He leads us by our feelings. As difficult as it may be for the more dramatic personalities among us to believe, individuals with phlegmatic, stoic personalities do hear from God. In fact, sometimes they hear more easily than the emotionally prone person does because they don't filter everything through their feelings.

We who are more emotional have to learn to separate emotional reactions from the anointing and the inner witness. God leads us by the inner witness of His Spirit, by His Word and by His peace:

> **For as many as are led by the Spirit of God, they are the sons of God**
>
> **Romans 8:14**

> **Thy word is a lamp unto my feet, and a light unto my path.**
> **Psalm 119:105**

> **And let the peace (soul harmony which comes) from Christ rule (act as umpire continually) in your hearts [deciding and settling with finality all questions that arise in your minds].**
> **Colossians 3:15** AMP

The writer of Hebrews asks: **Shall we not much rather be in subjection unto the Father of spirits?** (Heb. 12:9). God is a Spirit, and those who worship Him must do so in spirit and in truth. (John 4:24.)

In Romans 8:14, Paul gives us insight into how we are to relate to God, pointing out that those who are led by the Spirit of God are the true sons of God. Also, Romans 8:16 reveals that the Spirit Himself "bears witness" with our spirits—not our emotions—that we are the children of God.

Emotions are ever-changing; they are not dependable. Therefore, God deals with us Spirit to spirit.

Visions and Voices

God speaks to us through His Word and the internal witness of the Holy Spirit. Depending on visions and voices apart from the Word of God is dangerous and will lead to spiritual experiences that are not scripturally substantiated. A new believer who witnesses unscriptural manifestations can be easily misled. This can be especially detrimental when the Word of God is set aside.

For example, I once attended a prayer group in which a mother of two teenage sons shared with the rest of the group that her boys were out of control and her home was in a state of turmoil. Her anguish was heart-rending as she requested prayer. The group immediately began to pray in loud, thunderous, earnest prayer.

After a while, the lady fell to the floor. A young woman who seemed to be the leader of the group began to describe a beautiful casket dripping with jewels descending from heaven. As she finished relating her vision in grandiose language, the group exploded with excitement. The crescendo of praise was almost deafening, and then there was quiet.

A newcomer attempted to share Scripture that she believed would give hope, assurance and substance to the vision. She was quieted and told that Scriptures were not needed—the prayer had already been answered.

Obviously, this mother felt better. But faith cannot take root in the emotional realm of feelings. Faith is not "feeling better." **Faith cometh by hearing, and hearing by the word of God** (Rom. 10:17).

If the vision is from God, it can bear scrutiny, and the Word of God will confirm it. The Bible says in the mouth of two or three witnesses, let every word be established. (2 Cor. 13:1.)

In another group, a woman who attended regularly obviously had many problems in every area of her life. Yet invariably during praise and worship time, she would seemingly have a "word" from the Lord for the assembly. After the last amen, the leader knew at least one person would ask, "Is something wrong with me? When that woman speaks, I get very uncomfortable, but I don't know why. Is it my immaturity?"

The group leader didn't have the answer, so she waited on God to show her what to do. She didn't want to discourage anyone who was seeking to know more of God, but something was not right with these "manifestations" of the Spirit. The words seemed suitable, but they left a discomforting and disquieting atmosphere.

Which spirit was working here? Was it God? The woman giving the words certainly needed help—physically, mentally and spiritually. Incidentally, her finances were so bad that she had nowhere to live at times.

The leader believed with all her heart that they would see a transformation in this outspoken woman and that God would be glorified. So she continued to pray for her, asking the Holy Spirit for the discerning of spirits. Soon the leader realized that God was requiring her to take action. She hoped that there wouldn't be another word from this woman.

While preparing a lesson for the class, the leader's research took her to a passage in Acts 16. She had read and was rereading the account of the demon-possessed woman who followed Paul everywhere he went, saying, **These men are the servants of the most high God, which shew unto us the way of salvation** (Acts 16:17).

Visualizing Paul's experience as she read Acts 16 again, the leader saw her "internal picture" change, as God granted her discernment through a vision. She watched as Bible streets faded and her study group came into view. The young woman in Acts had a face she recognized: it was the woman in her prayer group. Then the leader knew that a spirit of divination was at work through this outspoken woman in the group.

During the next Bible study, the leader asked the woman to meet with her after the service. At their meeting, the leader asked her how she received her words from the Lord. The woman said she heard a voice telling her what to say. Many times she had written down the words ahead of time and meditated on them.

The leader shared with the woman that this was not God's voice and asked her if she wanted to be free to hear the voice of God.

"No!" she exclaimed. "This voice has talked to me since I was five years old and is my best friend. I find it difficult to read the Bible, so the voice tells me everything I need to know. I would have to give up all my journals, and I won't do that. They are the only thing I manage to salvage and keep with me at all times. I don't want 'deliverance'; I don't need deliverance." With that, she turned and walked away.

Do not be led astray by visions or voices, dear friend! God is not flaky, and He doesn't want His children acting improperly.

Some individuals have the idea that in order to be spiritual, one must act weird. But prayer isn't enigmatic or mystical. What is prayer? It is spiritual business governed by spiritual laws. And your "business partner" is God!

Fleshly Manifestations

A letter I once received from a prayer group leader described how two women in her group were operating within the group. When a prayer request was shared, one of the women would get down on her hands and knees, positioning herself to become a chalice for the evil spirits that were harassing the individual they were praying for. As she crawled around the room, her friend followed her, casting out evil spirits—even though the chalice turned to claw her legs again and again.

These two friends were sincere in their procedure, and their intentions were good. However, their bizarre behavior was creating confusion, uneasiness and apprehension in the prayer group. Believers who sincerely desired to learn more about prayer were distancing themselves from the group. The leader wanted to know how to deal wisely with all involved.

The Holy Spirit enabled the leader to see beyond the weird behavior to recognize the sincerity of these two women. They were willing to set aside personal dignity and be ridiculed if such fleshly manifestations would bring deliverance and salvation to those for whom they were praying.

Satan uses every device to stop prayer groups from praying prayers that avail much. In this case, he had taken advantage of wrong prayer ideas. When this prayer group leader sought counsel from her pastor, they decided to hold a seminar on prayer, and the situation was corrected. As John 8:32 (NKJV) says, **You shall know the truth, and the truth shall make you free.**

In Proverbs 2:1-6 (NIV), God exhorts us:

> **If you accept my words and store up my commands within you, turning your ear to wisdom and applying your heart to understanding, and if you call out for insight and cry aloud for understanding, and if you look for it as for silver and search for it as for hidden treasure, then you will understand the fear of the Lord and find the knowledge of God.**
>
> **For the Lord gives wisdom, and from his mouth come knowledge and understanding.**

God delights in answering prayer that is prayed according to His Word and His wisdom. Jesus said,

> **If you remain in me and my words remain in you, ask whatever you wish, and it will be given you. This is to my Father's glory, that you bear much fruit, showing yourselves to be my disciples.**
>
> **John 15:7,8 NIV**

Answered prayer glorifies the Father!

CHAPTER 7

Who Is Called To Pray?

A few years ago, after several strenuous days of ministering and taking care of my family, I walked out of what was for me a difficult meeting. Feeling drained and defeated, I complained loud and long to myself about the intercessors who obviously were not doing their job! *Had they been doing their job, I reasoned, my teaching and ministry would be going much more smoothly and easily.*

Learning a Lesson From Football

When I finally asked God for wisdom concerning this predicament, the Lord revealed something to me about the prayer responsibility of the speaker. That revelation came as the result of watching a football game, of all things.

Being the dutiful wife that I am, I had sat down in the living room with my husband to watch a football game on television. There I sat, asking all sorts of questions about the game, which my husband answered with measured patience.

I watched as big men in uniforms ran, slammed into each other, knocked one another down and fell all over each other. All of this was done for the sake of catching a ball that was either flying through the air or being kicked around until someone caught it or a group of players piled on top of it.

Then the Lord used the dynamics of football to show me how He holds each person responsible for his own personal prayer life.

It is amazing how busy we can become keeping appointments, preparing messages and ministering to both groups and individuals, all the while forgetting the most important meeting of all: our time with the Father.

In the football illustration God gave me, I saw that the linemen (the intercessors and those in the ministry of helps) get into position, ready to charge the opposing line and open a path for their backfield to break through. Behind them stands the quarterback (the apostle, prophet, evangelist, pastor and teacher) who is responsible for properly reading the defense and calling the correct offensive plays. If anyone on the team is out of position or fails to do his job, his actions affect all the other team members.

Regardless of how well the linemen play, since they neither call the plays nor carry the ball, they are limited in their capacity to win the game. Without the well-prepared, mentally alert, physically able-bodied quarterback, theirs is virtually an impossible task. And the quarterback cannot lead his team to victory without the proper preparation and willingness to accept and follow the instructions of his coach.

The light dawned! I acknowledged my sin of prayerlessness and repented for transferring personal blame and condemnation to my teammates, who are always faithful to pray for me. The real fault was mine for having neglected my privilege to spend time conferring directly with my "Divine Coach" so I could carefully follow His game plan.

God's Game Plan

The entire body of Christ, working together in harmony with the Holy Spirit and each other, will produce positive results. Every member of the body has a place in the church. Each individual is responsible for putting on the entire armor of God. Our foundation is the Word of God; our standard, the banner of love; our clothing, humility.

The quarterback cannot win the game by himself. He needs the team to work together shoulder to shoulder in an orderly array.

The apostle Paul compared the teamwork of the body of Christ to the function of a physical body in Ephesians 4:16 (AMP):

> **Because of Him [Jesus] the whole body (the church, in all its various parts), closely joined and firmly knit together by the joints and ligaments with which it is supplied, when each part [with power adapted to its need] is working properly [in all its functions], grows to full maturity, building itself up in love.**

At one end of the spectrum are those in the body of Christ who give little or no attention to prayer. At the other extreme are people who pray, separating themselves from others in the body of Christ.

As agents of prayer, we are to appropriate prayer as a lifestyle and welcome the accountability required of each person to carry his own load. Individually, we are parts of one another, mutually dependent on one another.

On one occasion, Jesus asked three of His disciples to come with Him to pray. However, in Luke 18:1 (AMP), Jesus indicated to us collectively that we **ought always to pray and not to turn coward (faint, lose heart, and give up).** Jesus also said to watch and pray so we would not enter into temptation. (Matt.26:41.) No one is immune to temptation, so this commandment includes all of us!

Successful apostles, prophets, evangelists, pastors and teachers are men and women who maintain an effective prayer life. Ideally, diverse members of the body have also answered the call to surround them in prayer. There is strength in numbers, for the Bible says that one shall put a thousand to flight, and two shall put ten thousand to flight. (Deut. 32:30.) However, the "quarterbacks" of the body of Christ should also maintain strong personal prayer lives themselves.

We can derive great benefit from studying the lives of successful people in the ministry, such as John Wesley, Andrew Murray, E. M. Bounds and Dr. Paul Cho, to name a few. However, Jesus should always remain our primary role model for leadership.

We stand in awe as we read the New Testament, viewing the past events of the miraculous public ministry of the man called Jesus. Yet we often fail to recognize the key to His success: Jesus was a person of prayer. He spent much time fellowshipping with the Father. How often we find that Jesus arose early in the day to spend time in prayer and fellowship with the Father.

I can't help but believe that much of Jesus' time in prayer with the Father concerned the fulfillment of Old Testament prophecy, as well as simply discussing the ways of God and receiving His instruction.

Anyone who experiences a satisfactory prayer life is a student of the Scriptures. Jesus spoke what He heard the Father say, and He did what He saw the Father do. Most of those times of prayer and communion Jesus spent in solitude, apart from even His intimate friends and disciples.

In Luke 11:1, we read that Jesus' disciples came to Him and asked Him to teach them to pray. Obviously they recognized that the source of His power emanated from His fellowship with the Father in prayer.

So often our own prayer time is controlled by needs. But crises didn't dictate the prayer life of Jesus. He prayed both before and after His times of public ministry. The results were evident.

It is reasonable to me that Jesus practiced what He taught. I imagine Him confidently asking the Father to fulfill His promises and prophecies for His sojourn on earth.

In his writings, Matthew's favorite word seems to be *fulfilled*. According to the accounts recorded in the gospels, Jesus did seek and discover the Father's will in all situations—where to go, where to speak, when to go and who to see. And just as He taught others to do, I believe that He knocked and it was opened to Him. He walked this earth as the Son of Man. He was tempted in all points just as we are, yet He was without sin.

The prayer life of Jesus bore fruit and gained renown, as we read in Acts 10:38 (AMP):

> **How God anointed and consecrated Jesus of Nazareth with the [Holy] Spirit and with strength and ability and power; how**

He went about doing good and, in particular, curing all who were harassed and oppressed by [the power of] the devil, for God was with Him.

It is almost beyond belief, but Jesus said we can perform the same works He did:

I assure you, most solemnly I tell you, if anyone steadfastly believes in Me, he will himself be able to do the things that I do; and he will do even greater things than these, because I go to the Father.

John 14:12 AMP

Why Aren't We More Successful
in Fulfilling God's Plan?

We have to ask ourselves: Why is the church not regularly and systematically producing these "greater works"? Could the answer be a failure to pray? Could the answer be that we are yet carnal, behaving as mere men, each of us insisting on our own way? The body of Christ is greater than our local church or denomination. Let us unite in prayer.

Prayer is something we can easily put off unless we make it as habitual as brushing our teeth. But after years of making prayer a lifestyle, today I would rather leave the house without brushing my teeth than leave without having prayed.

Personal procrastination leads to prayerlessness. This is a sin of which we must repent. Procrastination also results in anxiety and guilt. Sometimes we get so busy doing good works for God that we neglect our prayer time. He allows us to make our own decisions, but when we begin to feel overburdened or overtaxed, it is time to check our prayer life. Our priorities have simply gotten turned upside down.

Our own personal issues or the needs of others become so mountainous, we feel powerless—and we are. However, we know the One who is all-powerful.

So just as you would set aside time for any important function in your life, set aside a specific time to fellowship with the Father in the "inner chamber." If you don't feel like praying, just tell Him. He knows how to help you and draw you to His side, for no one comes to the place of prayer except the Father draws him.

According to many sources John Wesley said, "It seems God is limited by our prayer life, that He can do nothing for humanity unless someone ask Him." This statement reveals our joyous responsibility of praying that the will of God might be done on earth as it is in heaven.

When Jesus prayed, the supernatural pervaded the natural, the heavens opened and the will of God was revealed as the natural was changed into the supernatural and the Father was glorified. However, in Jesus' hour of greatest need, He called three of His closest disciples to accompany Him, requesting that they stay awake and pray.

Sadly, Jesus' disciples failed Him, just as we often do. (Matt. 26:37-46.) How sad that the Holy Spirit has to pass us by and look for another person who will submit to His gentle nudging to pray!

I know that in order for churches and ministries to accomplish the work of the Lord in this day, they need the prayerful aid and support of others. Many pastors personally lead their intercessors in organized prayer rather than appointing someone else to lead a prayer group. Ideally, the entire church makes up a prayer group. Large churches often have numerous prayer groups specializing in different aspects of prayer. The pastor can either himself train others to be leaders of these prayer groups, or he can have a trusted leader conduct the training.

It is necessary that a minister maintain close contact with the prayer group leader by giving (and receiving) wise counsel. A group that is led by the pastor himself has direct counsel and knowledge of the specific areas of concern in the church. So often the pastor is aware of details that the intercessors may need to know.

A common mistake made by some ministers is that of depending solely on one or two people to pray and hear from God for the direction of the ministry. When this happens, the responsibility for the church guidance shifts from the God-appointed leader to a member of the flock.

In this type of situation, the other person is placed in a position to dominate and usurp authority, often falling into the error of controlling another's ministry in a very subtle manner. When control issues and power plays become the focus, the results are detrimental.

So often we fail in our churches because we do not wait on the plan of God or follow divine authority. There are those who have been given authority to oversee the spiritual growth of their church membership. When this responsibility is transferred to others, both pastors and laymen can be wounded.

Many of us have escaped rigid religious backgrounds where we have been under the control and sway of man's traditions and dogmas. Renewal movements bring life, and with them, freedom and deliverance from religious bondage. I have observed that in past moves of God, we sometimes acted like children turned loose in a candy factory. We gorged ourselves until we became satiated with power and zeal, without understanding the responsibilities that accompany deliverance. Our maturity attained is indeed only another phase of growth. More growth awaits us.

Some have believed that no one but the Holy Spirit should be designated as "head" of any assembly. Others desire godly leaders, but when these leaders began to exercise their God-given license to make decisions, problems arise among those who do not want to follow.

This is not new. Moses was a target of disgruntled, rebellious people. The issue of who is in control opens the door to clashes and conflicts. Within these conditions, hidden personal agendas are exposed, misunderstandings arise and people of opposing views may or may not communicate by refusing to listen to one another.

Communication is confused because of wrong mind-sets. We begin establishing strongholds to protect our wrong attitudes and motives, thinking,

I am right because I hear from God, and you are wrong. Leaders are given ultimatums: "If you don't do as I say, I will take my ball and bat and go home."

Ministry leaders with unresolved issues, unmet needs and unhealed hurts also pass out their own ultimatums. Accusations are thrown at one another, and unscriptural terms such as "spirit of control" or "Jezebel spirit" become nasty, hateful expressions. Misunderstandings result from people's own personal interpretations. Authority is misused when power is abused.

Support and Submission
to Those in Authority

The ministry leader is the overseer on earth under the direction of the Holy Spirit. Does this leader sometimes make mistakes? Certainly!

God sends people to uphold and support the leader's vision by fulfilling the everyday tasks of activating and performing the work of the ministry. But it is inevitable that at times uncomfortable decisions will have to be faced. If everyone will just be patient and stay where God has planted him or her, the Lord will work out the situation for the good of the ministry and of everyone else involved.

You see, God has given us the responsibility to **strive earnestly to guard and keep the harmony and oneness of [and produced by] the Spirit in the binding power of peace** (Eph. 4:3 AMP). Will we pass our test, even though it may be uncomfortable? Are we willing to let go of our strongholds of rigidity, emotional isolation, silence and denial? Or do we build walls with words, leaving no room for discussion lest we have to submit to the constant transformation of the Holy Spirit?

Where a leader is weak, God will provide strength through the talents and abilities of others. The apostle Paul said, **Now I am glad to boast about how weak I am; I am glad to be a living demonstration of Christ's power, instead of showing off my own power and abilities** (2 Cor. 12:9 TLB).

The ability to delegate and trust others to do their jobs is very difficult for some leaders. When they see a department succeeding, they may view it as a potential threat to their leadership.

But God often uses people as one of His resources to supply the strength that is most needed. It is the responsibility of the leader to receive and channel these "gifts" for the good of the ministry and to the glory of God. Those called alongside the pastor or leader will act as Aarons and Hurs to assist and to serve. (Ex. 17:8-13.)

Everyone is important in the body of Christ, and everyone will reap the rewards of a job well done. We need the fivefold ministry gifts just as much as we need the ministry of helps, which includes intercessors. We need one another.

Don't Usurp the Holy Spirit's Role
in People's Lives

In certain circumstances, ministers and lay people alike may unwittingly violate each other's boundaries, treading on ground where angels fear to tread.

For instance, sometimes instead of taking responsibility for our own actions, we may become self-appointed censors of other people's behavior. When that happens, phrases such as "God told me that you..." or "God said that you should..." or "God showed me that you are being controlled by an evil spirit" are often used to great excess. In the process, new Christians are wounded.

Often we are puzzled when others don't joyfully receive the "word" we received from the Lord for them. We are amazed to discover that they are even hurt by that word. We may attempt to justify our actions by saying, "After all, I'm only obeying God."

But could it be that the word from God was for our personal emotional healing and spiritual growth? It may be that God was entrusting us with a word concerning a person for whom we were praying. These words from God are to be held in trust for the purpose of prayer.

We walk worthy of our divine call to pray by waiting for God to bring revelation to an individual. We are not to usurp the authority of the Holy Ghost to lead and guide in a person's life.

Most of the time, it is better to be quiet about your prayers for others. At times, however, God may want you to share what you have learned. Wait for confirmation that you are praying accurately. Also, wait for God's appointed time to share. He is not only preparing you but the heart of the person for whom you are praying to receive encouragement, correction or instruction.

When we hurt others, we sometimes attribute their pain to their immaturity because we are convinced that mature Christians cannot be hurt emotionally. But that just isn't true. We must acknowledge our mistakes and accept responsibility by asking for forgiveness without offering any excuses.

Unfortunately, some wounded hearts may be lost to us. Proverbs 18:19 (NIV) says, **A brother offended is harder to be won than a strong city: and their contentions are like the bars of a castle.** In these situations, we must pray to be restorers of the streets where we dwell.

Biblical Resolution of Conflict
Within the Local Church

Both pastors and church members must learn how to correctly handle conflicts and problems that arise within the church. At times, an emotionally crippled pastor takes advantage of the pulpit to try to "fix" those giving him problems. Wounded members feel exposed and receive the pastor's messages as degrading and insulting. The doors of the church turn into revolving doors. People exit as quickly as they enter, defeating church growth and hindering evangelism. Both long-standing members and visitors feel the dysfunction in the atmosphere.

In an effort to keep everything together while they search for answers, ministers sometimes unknowingly try to control the congregation and events from the pulpit. On the other hand, intercessors are often convinced that enough prayer will save those who are causing trouble, and they move into an area of prayerful manipulation. Accusations fly back and forth like a tennis game—and it is all in the name of the Lord!

In such situations, new wounds are opened, old wounds are reopened and carnal emotional and psychological patterns of protection return. Strongholds are reinforced, and everyone involved remains emotionally isolated from each other.

In the pressure of this atmosphere, an overloaded pastor welcomes a willing heart that commits to pray and lead others in prayer. It is a relief to share the responsibility of hearing from God with others.

Many believe that prayer alone can resolve any issue, forgetting that faith without actions is dead. Prayer prepares the way for an encounter, but it is no substitute for resolving conflict when face-to-face encounters are needed. This type of encounter requires honest, open discussion, a listening ear and an intense desire to understand another person's viewpoint.

Author Jesse Penn-Lewis offers the following practical suggestion:

> When you are working with another and you do not see "eye to eye" mentally, you can still be of *one spirit* if you walk after the spirit. Understand this, and you will delight in discovering all the different points of view God gives His children. God is the only One with an infinite mind. If you remember that you have only a *finite* mind, you will not want everyone to see eye to eye with you in everything.[1]

If we are to develop healthy relationships within our church families, we have to practice walking in the light. In God's presence, we learn to esteem others, and our respect for ourselves will be reflected in our respect for others. Then we will have wonderful fellowship and joy with each other as the blood of Jesus His Son cleanses us from every sin. (1 John 1:7.)

As a church family, we need to honestly acknowledge our flaws and our shortcomings, making ourselves accountable. We must also obey God's

admonition to pray for one another that we may all be restored to a spiritual tone of mind and heart. (James 5:16 AMP.)

Control issues must be resolved, or the results will be detrimental to
both the ministry and the intercessor. It is not the responsibility of the team
members to make decisions apart from the leadership.

When the church intercessor accepts the responsibility of hearing from
God for a church or any other ministry—whether that responsibility is self-
imposed or delegated by the ministry leader—lines of authority become
confused. People in the congregation don't know who to look to as their
spiritual authority.

Regardless of our position in the church—minister or prayerful layper-
son—we are to resist a prideful attitude. Instead of thinking of ourselves
more highly than we should, we must clothe ourselves in humility.

James 3:13 (NIV) reveals that the wise and intelligent person will show
forth his good works with unobtrusive humility, which is the very opposite
of pride. Pride seems to be common to us all. Far too often we become
prideful and stumble over our own imposed importance.

There is an established line of authority in the church. When that
authority is violated, Satan (who is a shrewd legalist) takes advantage of the
situation. We may blame our stressful situation on the devil, but it is our
own stubbornness and self-will that gives him space to operate.

Leadership and laity must work out their individual salvation, knowing
that the engrafted word is able to save their souls. *It is the unresolved issues
of the soul that divide us, not the things of the Spirit of God.*

Wisdom from above prepares and equips believers to operate according to the divine chain of command. A pastor or ministry leader who accepts
and retains his God-given privilege and responsibility of spiritual leadership will nurture within his congregation a sense of safety and security.

Regardless of the ministry focus of a church, prayer is the foundation of
its success. Honesty requires us to confess our shortcomings and sins to
God and to one another. We are to pray for one another that we may all be

healed and restored to a spiritual tone of mind and heart. Earnest, heartfelt prayer will produce results. Therefore, let us learn true submission and submit one to the other.

Stay Within Scriptural Boundaries
of Intercession

An effective prayer group operates in wisdom from above. People who respond in godly wisdom yield to reason, demonstrate compassion and produce good fruits, always walking in the love of God. Cognizant of their prayerful alliance to their Father God, to their pastor and to the congregation, intercessors who operate according to divinely established order will not attempt to assume the responsibility of the pastor.

A group of ladies began meeting together to pray for their pastor. It wasn't too many weeks before they "heard from God" for him. They targeted certain individuals, calling them demon-possessed and future troublemakers and demanding that the pastor turn them out of the church.

These were women who loved the Lord and truly wanted to be used by God. But they were operating in the flesh and out of their own soulish interpretations.

The pastor wisely refused to comply with their demands. But rather than respond in a spiritually mature manner and allow God to direct their pastor, the intercessors became outraged and self-righteous in their attitude and actions.

They believed that God was showing them all their pastor's flaws and shortcomings. For one thing, he was watching too much television, they decided. They prayed more diligently to bring about a change in his everyday conduct based on their unfounded judgments of him.

No matter how anointed the pastor's sermons were, these women were convinced that they were right about him. When he refused to act on their revelations, they believed he was in open disobedience to God's will. Their denial and support of one another as intercessors rendered them unable to see their dictatorial, overbearing attitude toward their pastor. They under-estimated his spirituality while overestimating theirs. Finally, the women chose to leave the church, loudly protesting their pastor's decision, convinced they were right.

These women slipped into the snare of pride. Perhaps they believed they were operating in the discerning of spirits, the gift of the Spirit referred to in 1 Corinthians 12:9 that operates as the Spirit of God wills.

However, true godly discernment never becomes the personal "posses-sion" or prerogative of the individual through whom it operates. This belief is a deception that gives way to a critical and judgmental attitude.

In his book, *Questions and Answers on Spiritual Gifts*, Howard Carter points out:

> There are those who have, perhaps unconsciously, criticized their brethren, and have believed they were manifesting this gift [the discerning of spirit] when they supposedly detected "demon power" in nearly every meeting they have entered. They profess to see demon power in the services, demon influences moving the speaker, demon spirits everywhere. They have accounted for every lack of blessing by demon power only, and they have seen nothing by their supposed exercise of the gift by what has been bad.[2]

Constantly looking for problems and inadequacies in every situation leads to operating in negativism instead of in the power of the Holy Spirit. Similarly, focusing on demons attracts demons. Jesus directs our focus in Luke 10:20 (NAB): **Do not rejoice because the spirits are subject to you, but rejoice because your names are written in heaven.**

The time has come for the entire church to answer the call to prayer. God called us to keep the unity of the Spirit through the bond of peace. (Eph. 4:3.) Prayer will usher the church of Jesus Christ into the unity of the faith under the direction of God-appointed leadership. Scriptural prayers issuing from pure hearts in an atmosphere of harmony and agreement will avail much.

Begin to practice the presence of God in your personal life at home and at work. Make a conscious and consistent decision to honor God by submitting to one another. To submit to authority is not a hindrance or restriction; it is protection. Submission and humility provide a check-and-balance system that frustrates strife and division while promoting agreement.

In the church at Philippi, two women in positions of leadership were of differing opinions, and the opportunity for strife and conflict was evident. Paul instructed the church to help these two women to keep on cooperating, pointing out that they had toiled along with him in the spreading of the Gospel.

Paul prayed diligently and consistently for the churches. His prayers always focused on spiritual development and emotional wholeness. Prayer prepared the believers to receive instructions on how to get along with one another here in this world environment.

Paul also admonished the church to pray:

> **Pray at all times (on every occasion, in every season) in the Spirit, with all [manner of] prayer and entreaty. To that end keep alert and watch with strong purpose and perseverance, interceding in behalf of all the saints (God's consecrated people). And [pray] also for me, that [freedom of] utterance may be given me, that I may open my mouth to proclaim boldly the mystery of the good news (the Gospel).**
>
> **Ephesians 6:18 AMP**

Although there are certain called-out ones who serve as intercessors in the church, we are all called to a lifestyle of prayer. In Matthew 21:13 (AMP), Jesus noted, The Scripture says, **My house shall be called a house of prayer.** Individually, each of us is a temple of the Holy Spirit, or a house of prayer. Together, we make up one great household of prayer. (Eph. 2:20-22.)

When each one of us assumes our respective position on the team esteeming one another, miracles will take place, the plan of God will unfold and we will become one in Christ Jesus—then the world will know that God the Father has sent His Son for their salvation. In this the Father is glorified!

CHAPTER 8

Preparing for Intercession

J esus taught us to plan. No one builds a house without planning and counting the cost. Praying for others will cost us time, effort and energy. Preparation is necessary for every worthwhile endeavor.

God obviously had a plan when He created the heavens and the earth. When you observe nature—the sun, moon, stars and planets—it isn't difficult to recognize the craftsmanship of a master builder.

But consider this: You were included in this master plan. God knew you and chose you before the foundation of the world. When you commit your ways to the Lord, He causes your thoughts to become agreeable to His will. Then *your* plans are established and destined to succeed. (Prov. 16:3 AMP.)

Is there a God-ordained plan and structure for intercessory prayer and for prayer groups? Yes! If we look at ourselves as God's army of intercessors, we realize that there are times of spiritual warfare. We are the enforcers of the triumphant victory of Jesus Christ. It is up to each of us to determine his or her own position and responsibility as an agent of prayer.

Jesus is the Head of the church. Without Him, we can do nothing. If we remain in Him and His words remain in us, we can ask whatever you wish, and it will be given us. In this the Father is glorified. (John 15:7 NIV.)

The secret is abiding in Jesus and keeping His words alive and living in you. His Word reveals your position in this activity called intercessory prayer.

Agents of Prayer

Today Jesus is physically seated at the right hand of the Father in heavenly places,

> **...far above all principality, and power, and might, and dominion, and every name that is named, not only in this age, but also in that which is to come. And [God] put all things under his feet, and gave Him to be the head over all things to the church, which is his body, the fulness of Him who fills all in all.**
>
> **Eph. 1:21-23**

This position honors Jesus as the One who has been given all authority both in heaven and earth. (Matt. 28:18.)

God raised you up together with Christ and made you sit down together with Him in the heavenlies far above powers and principalities. (Eph. 1:20,21.) This "far above" gives you the authority to act as an agent of the Lord Jesus Christ by the will of God here on planet earth.

God's plan for us as agents of Jesus Christ is for us to pray. This admonition is scattered throughout the Bible. Along with the joyous responsibility of prayer, He has given you the authority to pray *effectively.*

When Jesus walked the earth, He revealed the impotency of Satan in the presence of God. He went about doing good and healing all who were oppressed by the devil. (Acts 10:38.)

Some time ago, the Lord graciously gave me a dream that illustrates the intrusion of Satan against the church. In my dream, I walked into my gleaming white kitchen and saw what appeared to be an army of common house roaches advancing toward me. Naturally, I recoiled. At the same time, I realized these were no ordinary roaches but vile little creatures with different-colored bodies that flashed like neon lights.

Immediately and unexpectedly, strength surged up from my inner being, and I thought, "Why, I *refuse* to shrink back! I can step on each one of these and destroy them."

With newfound courage, I changed my tactic from retreat to attack. As I advanced toward the loathsome creatures, stomping my feet with great fervor, they ran from me, slithering under the back door. Just then, I awoke with a solid understanding of the dream's message: Do not be afraid of the devil!

Upon awakening, the words of Jesus sounded loud and clear in my spirit,

Behold, I give unto you power to tread on serpents and scorpions, and over all the power of the enemy: and nothing shall by any means hurt you

Luke 10:19

Notice that Jesus made this statement *before* He went to the Cross and before He stripped principalities and powers, making a show of them openly. Jesus walked this earth as a victor. He was victorious over the enemy.

So never back away from the enemy or go on the defensive. Take your stand, and having done all to stand, stand, enforcing the triumphant victory of our leader, our Lord Jesus Christ. (Col. 2:15.)

Praying With Joy

God has not called you to a wearisome, irksome task. He has called you to a life of powerful communion with Him. Strategy for spiritual warfare issues from the throne room of God. Living a lifestyle of prayer and practicing the presence of Jesus is joy unspeakable and full of glory.

Paul writes in Phil. 1:4 (AMP), **In every prayer of mine I always make my entreaty and petition for you all with joy (delight).** The Father is your exceeding great joy (Ps. 43:4), and He desires that you deliberately enter into His presence where you can undergo an infusion of His life.

Each and every day, make a decision to enjoy the privilege of entering into true communion with God the Father, Jesus our Lord and the Holy Spirit.

The Key to God's Heart

Moses was an intercessor who seemed to know how to communicate with God. Their conversations are recorded to be an example for us. Moses found grace in the sight of the Lord and declared he would not go on unless the presence of God went with him. God promised to go with Moses and give him rest. (Ex. 33:14.)

Just as Moses required the presence of God to go with him, we, too, need God's presence to go with us into spiritual conflicts. Moses found the key to reach the heart of God. That key is to commune with the Father, Spirit to spirit, every day.

Psalm 100:

A Blueprint for Devotions

We are not prepared to meet the day or the challenges we may face until we have entered into sweet communion with the Holy Ghost. Psalm 100 might be used as a structure for private devotions, for it provides a blueprint for passage into the presence of God.

First, it says, **Shout for joy to the Lord, all the earth.** Regardless of what your circumstances may be, start your day or any time of prayer with praise to the Lord! Your feelings may betray you. They may even attempt to overwhelm and quench your joy. But joy is not an emotion; joy is a fruit of the spirit. Joy is a spiritual force that is always available to help you confront your feelings of disappointment, depression, oppression, bad feelings toward others, self-pity and other negative thought patterns.

The Bible says that happy are the people whose God is the Lord. Acknowledge your feelings, be honest and do not try to gloss over or hide your feelings from God.

My mother taught us children that we have the power of choice. Well, it takes a made-up mind to praise the Lord. So choose to praise Him just because of who He is! Praise Him even though your expressions may sound hollow, mechanical and void of sincerity. Declare with the psalmist David, "While I have breath, I will praise my God." (Ps. 150:6.) As you do, your praise will take on substance.

Worship the Lord with gladness; come before Him with joyful songs. When you delight yourself in the Lord, your desires correspond to His, causing you to delight in keeping His commandments. The Lord's commandments are neither grievous nor burdensome. He has made us glad.

So sing Mary's song: "My soul does magnify the Lord, and my spirit does rejoice in God my Savior." (Luke 1:46,47.) Come into His presence with singing, for He has put a new song in your heart. Release gladness in words and music.

Again, do not look for your emotions to confirm your glad heart. Lay your burdens at His feet and praise Him. He has given you beauty for ashes, the oil of joy for mourning, and the garment of praise for a spirit of heaviness. (Isa. 61:3.)

Thirdly, know that the Lord is God. It is he, who made us, and we are his; we are his people, the sheep of his pasture. Prayer is based on relationship. Therefore, if our prayers are to be effective, we must know our God. The many different names of God reveal His nature and character.[1]

Not only must you know Him, but you must know who you are in Him. Understand your position through identification with Christ. You are an agent of the Lord Jesus Christ by the will of God, an agent filled with His grace and peace.

You are blessed with all spiritual blessings. You were chosen before the foundation of the world. You are holy and without blame before Him in love. You are redeemed through His blood. You are accepted in the beloved. You are God's child through Jesus Christ. You are an agent of wisdom and understanding.

You were included in Christ when you heard the Word of Truth, the gospel of your salvation. You are marked with a seal, the promised Holy

Spirit. You are God's possession. (Eph. 1:1-14.) You are God's handiwork, recreated in Christ Jesus—His very own workmanship.

Grow more intimately acquainted with God. Know Christ and the power of His resurrection and the fellowship of his sufferings. (Phil. 3:10.) Knowing God and knowing yourself will build confidence toward God and faith in the ability of God within you to pray effectively.

Fourth, Enter his gates with thanksgiving and his courts with praise; give thanks to him and praise his name. Eulogize God. Speak of His wondrous love and mercy. Say good things about Him, for He has blessed you with all spiritual blessings in Christ. There is so much to be thankful for: **Thanks be to God for his indescribable gift!** (2 Cor. 9:15 NIV).

According to *Unger's Bible Dictionary:*

> The ethical gratitude of Christianity connects every good gift and every perfect gift with the gift of Christ. Moreover, it is a thanksgiving which in the Christian economy, and in it alone, redounds to God for all things: *in every-thing give thanks.*[2]

Thanksgiving is a privilege that will displace wrong perceptions about others. Thanksgiving will uproot denial and enable us to move out of emotional isolation to true intimacy. Strongholds that hinder intimacy with God are destroyed when we praise Him. Our God is an awesome God!

It is a privilege to thank God in all things, for this is the will of God in Christ Jesus concerning us. Praise is the sacrifice we offer as a symbol of communion between God and us, His children. The Holy Spirit perfects the fruit of our lips giving praise. Praise that flows from a grateful heart stops and stills the avenger! Satan is a defeated foe!

For the Lord is good and his love endures forever; his faithfulness continues through all generations (Psalm 100:5). Believe, and you and your household will be saved. (Acts 16:31.) His goodness and mercy shall follow you and your children all the days of your lives.

So often we focus on generational curses. But Jesus was made a curse for us. (Gal. 3:13.) Now we have the power to reverse patterns of destruction in our families.

Ask the Holy Spirit to reveal behaviors that identify your role in the games people play. Your role in your family was developed long ago, but you have the power of choice. Your behavior will change as you put on the Lord Jesus Christ. You will learn to respond as a peacemaker rather than react emotionally in familial situations.

Be a reconciler. Form habits that result in blessings. Speak words of grace to your family members. Generational *blessings* are also transferred from generation to generation! Look for those blessings. Believe that the Lord is good. Believe that His love endures forever and His faithfulness continues throughout the generations to your children, their children and their children's children.

Following this outline will bring you into the inner chamber, the Holy of Holies. There in the presence of God, you will find fullness of joy and pleasures forevermore. You will receive healing and rest for your soul. Your spirit, soul and body will unite, empowering you to love God with your entire being.

During times of praise and worship, God will communicate new ideas, bring understanding to life's enigmas and release the anointing to heal brokenness.

For instance, it was during a worship service at the church where we attended that the Holy Spirit revealed a scene from my childhood that had left me wounded for years.

With eyes closed, I stood in the presence of God, feeling lonely and grief-stricken. Rather than rebuking the acuteness of the pain, I flowed with emotions that were almost tangible.

You see, emotions are God-given. Just as physical pain alerts you to dysfunction in the body, emotional pain alerts you to dysfunction in the soul.

On this occasion, my emotions were letting me know that something was amiss in that part of my being called the soul. I was in the presence of God; the anointing to heal was pervasive, and I sensed that something wonderful was about to take place. This present suffering could not be compared to the glory that was about to take place.

For the first time, I recognized and acknowledged the truth: "Lord, I miss my sister. I wish that Frieda were here with me. Why did she have to die in that freak accident?" Tears began to stream down my face, and I released the grief that I had carried since I was a little girl.

The death of my baby sister was a bizarre accident that had left me riddled with guilt. My parents had stepped out of the room, and I was alone with my sister when she died. She fell head first into a bucket of water. Even though I'd had my back to her and didn't know she had fallen, I blamed myself for her death and wished that I had died in her place.

The consequence of this emotional scar was a sense of overwhelming shame. I had failed my parents. So before I was three years old, I had assumed the responsibility for their happiness. Satan used unresolved issues surrounding this loss to build a stronghold of emotional isolation, self-doubt and perfectionism. I believed that I could earn my right to live if I performed well, but my performance was never good enough.

After fifty years, I finally let go of my childish thought: *If I had died instead of my sister, my parents would be happy again and their world would be made perfect.*

In that very moment, I realized that the stronghold of shame and condemnation was destroyed and I no longer blamed myself for my sister's death. As I stood there, tears flowing, in the presence of God, I was set free from a past memory and its power to control me.

Receive *your* healing and deliverance as the Holy Spirit ministers to you. Dance before your King; put off burdens and heavy loads. Put on your garment of praise, and make a joyful noise to the Lord with gladness of heart! Sing a new song to Him. Let His praise be continually in your mouth.

All of this is preparation for intercession. Don't wait until you are in your prayer group to prepare for intercession. Begin this preparation at home in your private devotions. Make the decision to spend time with Jesus *before* you come together with the others in your prayer group

When Peter and John walked the streets of Jerusalem, the people could tell they had been with Jesus. In the same way, the key to our doing the works of Jesus is personal communion with God in the secret place.

When you pray in secret, God will reward you openly. The fruit of the spirit will be developed as you practice godly behavior, and you will influence others positively. The light in your eyes will make the hearts of others rejoice.

What does your countenance reveal about your internal attitudes and realities? Do you feel heavy-laden? Prayer assignments are not intended to become cares and worries. Do you walk around with a sad countenance? God is the health of your countenance; He is your exceeding great joy! So if you are burdened, listen to the words of Jesus:

> **Come to Me, all you who labor and are heavy-laden and overburdened, and I will cause you to rest. [I will ease and relieve and refresh your souls.] For My yoke is wholesome (useful, good— not harsh, hard, sharp, or pressing, but comfortable, gracious, and pleasant), and My burden is light and easy to be borne.**
>
> Matt. 11:28,30 AMP

You can be the most joyous person on earth, because in His presence is fullness of joy; at His right hand there are pleasures forevermore. (Ps. 16:11.)

By entering into a time of praise and worship using Psalm 100 as a model, each person has the opportunity to lay aside thoughts that interfere with being in full accord and of one harmonious mind and intention. (Phil. 2:2.) Praise stills the avenger while preparing intercessors for a united front in spiritual warfare.

Maintain Unity of the Spirit

Remember your stance in this warfare. You are the enforcer of a victory that has already been won!

In the place of prayer, God imparts His love to us and enables us to live, talk, walk and breathe love. Love is the foundation of intercessory prayer.

We have the privilege of becoming skillful in prayer through Bible study, prayer and meditation. But it is of vital importance that our prayer groups attain and maintain the unity of the Spirit. Love becomes our law, and we speak accordingly, doing everything in harmony with this royal law called love.

Jesus emphasized the necessity of achieving harmony in Matt. 18:19 AMP:

> **Again I tell you, if two of you shall agree on earth (harmonize together, make a symphony together) about whatever [anything and everything] they may ask, it will come to pass and be done for them by My Father in heaven.**

Recently, this passage of Scripture was beautifully illustrated to me in a romantic setting. My husband reserved a table for us at an upscale restaurant in downtown Atlanta. After dinner, we enjoyed the walk along the sidewalks of the city with its bright lights and bustling traffic. It was exciting to hear the laughter of joyful people—some rushing about while others strolled arm in arm.

Much too soon, we reached our destination, arriving early for a concert at Symphony Hall. People are fascinating to me, so I watched as the audience was ushered in to take their seats. To my delight, a musician appeared on stage, seemingly oblivious of the sparsely filled auditorium that would soon be packed with avid music lovers.

Then the lone violinist began to play and fine-tune his instrument. It was a pleasant enough sound. But in a few minutes, the stage filled with other musicians and their instruments. The sound was no longer pleasant, as each musician was an island unto himself, doing his own thing on his particular instrument.

Called-out greetings among friends, laughter and talking from the gathering audience combined with the noise of many instruments to fill the atmosphere. The crescendo of loud voices, the tinkling discordant sounds from some instruments, as well as the crashing, blasting, clanging, noisy sounds from other instruments became very unpleasant to the ear.

Just as I thought that the cacophony would consume me, quietness reigned. The maestro stood before us and took a bow as united thunderous applause broke forth. Everyone's eyes were riveted to this man with the baton. Musicians were at full attention. When the maestro lifted his baton, their instruments were in readiness. The concert began, and melodious sounds of heavenly music floated from the stage.

I closed my eyes and breathed into my being streams of living, gentle, silvery notes that surely flowed from the heart of God. At times, bolts of reverberations thundered through the airwaves. The music talked to us, bringing life, joy, peace, rest and blessed quietness to my soul.

Sometimes our hearts were so stirred that it was difficult to sit still any longer. The harpists waited patiently for their short passage; they had only a few measures to perform. The percussionists sat behind the others, waiting for that moment when the baton would signal their introduction. All members of the orchestra followed the lifting and pointing movements of the maestro's baton.

How was this harmony achieved? One thing that I noted immediately was that the performers were submissive to the conductor for the good of the entire group. It was also obvious that each performer knew his own instrument. It was synergy—fellowship, communion and agreement—in action.

After all, the musicians had practiced for years at home and in the studio where they had fine-tuned their skills. They had developed their musical abilities as near to perfection as possible. They were prepared. Each knew his part and the musical score, and each followed the conductor who led the orchestra.

As colaborers together with God, we also have a conductor. He is ever-present with us. He also appoints leaders who are His "under conductors."

But even though God sends others to equip you, there is a maestro with you at all times. He is that One who comes along beside you, instructing, teaching, leading, directing and even correcting in His own gentle way.

Jesus promised that He would be in our midst when we meet in His name. Nevertheless, preparation for corporate prayer requires study, adhering to sound doctrines and practicing at home or in small groups.

There is a time for praise and worship and a time for prayer—supplications, petitions and intercessions. Remember your God-given assignment when you come together. Keep in mind, too, that on occasion the Holy Spirit may direct you to a temporary assignment for that particular time.

The symphony does not always give the same performance; concerts vary from event to event. The musicians are ready in season and out of season to play the music of various composers.

In our prayer group, we receive prayer requests from people around the world. It is our spiritual responsibility to pray for them with the same fervency that we would pray for our own concerns. We prepare to enter into the concert of prayer under the leadership of our Conductor, and we trust Him to direct the prayer group leader. As a general rule, we lay aside self-serving thoughts and personal situations.

We are many members in one body of Christ, each having a different function. Just as God gave the priests of the Old Testament their assignments, so today He gives each of us certain directives in prayer.

No one person or group can carry all the needs of the people. The multitude of tasks require that each one takes his place in the body of Christ.

Principles of Scriptural Prayer

The keys of binding and loosing are useful in your preparation. Pray for your appointed leader and other group members, binding minds to the mind of Christ, that each may hold the thoughts, feelings and purposes of His heart. Loose minds from wrong attitudes of selfishness, wrong motives, wrong thought patterns of judging those who have submitted prayer requests and from obsessive analyzing of the situations.

God is not holding the people's trespasses against them, and neither should we. In His presence, it is easy to let this same attitude and purpose and humble mind be in us that was also in Christ Jesus. (Phil. 2:5 AMP.)

Unite with the Lord in His intercession, praying for the poor in spirit, those in captivity, the blind, the oppressed and those who are downtrodden, bruised, crushed and broken by calamity. Pray for others according to the will of God, preparing the way for them to know and enjoy their God-given destiny:

Go through, go through the gates! Prepare the way for the people. Cast up, cast up the highway! Gather out the stones. Lift up a standard or ensign over and for the peoples.

Isaiah 62:10

Jesus was wounded for their transgressions, and He was bruised for their iniquities. Jesus bore the sins and sorrows of many, and by the stripes that crisscrossed His back, they are healed.

So lift up the standard for all to see:

Behold, your salvation comes [in the person of the Lord]; behold, His reward is with Him, and His work and recompense before Him. And they shall call them the Holy People, the Redeemed of the Lord; and you shall be called Sought Out, a City Not Forsaken.

Isaiah 62:11,12 AMP

The beginning of these verses in Isaiah 62 give divine authorization for the believer to go through the gates! I like to link this statement with Jesus' statement: "The gates of hell shall not prevail against My church." (Matt. 16:18.)

With this in mind, pray for others as the Holy Spirit directs, remembering that He does not lead apart from the Word of God. Learn to recognize the voice of the Good Shepherd. There are many voices vying for your attention besides God's voice, such as the voices of need, of expectation and of emotions.

Some people say that God has never spoken to them, but He has through the pages of sixty-six books that are bound into two volumes: the Old and New Testaments. God's Word will endure forever.

We must never add to God's will by reading into the Scriptures something they do not say. As newborn Christians, we are to desire the sincere milk of the Word. But sometimes in our immaturity, we misinterpret its true meaning.

There is a small word in Psalm 37:4 that we ignore: **Delight thyself *also* in the Lord; and he shall give thee the desires of thine heart.** *Also* means in addition to. In other words, delighting ourselves in the Lord is only one of a list of instructions in this chapter that we are to follow.

Much too often this one verse has been misapplied to justify our selfishness and self-centeredness. But in reality, as we act on God's Word and delight ourselves in the Lord, our will is rendered flexible and pliable in the Master's hand. That's why Romans 12:2 says, **Do not be conformed to this world, but be transformed by the renewing of your mind.**

His Word removes selfish desires and wrong motives, replacing them with His good, acceptable and perfect will. Your desires are molded into His desires. He is all the while effectually at work in you, energizing and creating in you the power and the desire both to will and work for His good pleasure, satisfaction and delight. (Phil. 2:13 AMP.)

Our petitions, supplications and intercessions are to issue from a heart of selflessness. Prayer for others is rooted and grounded in the royal law of love. This love is a fruit of the spirit and has been shed abroad in our hearts by the Holy Spirit who has been given unto us. (Rom. 5:5.) As we grow spiritually, our emotional, egotistical desires are displaced.

God is merciful, and He knows the end from the beginning. In taking our first prayer steps, we often allow unhealed hurts, unmet needs and unresolved issues to cloud our prayers. We are unsure about our motives but have an intense desire to walk in emotional wholeness and soundness.

As we continue to work out our salvation, the Holy Spirit comes to our aid and support, bearing us up in our inability to produce desired results. He helps us when we do not know how to pray or for what to pray.

In the privacy of our closet time with God, sins, weaknesses and character flaws are exposed. Even though we are unable to change ourselves in our own strength, the power of God produces changes in us—as long as we are willing to submit to the ministry of transformation by the Holy Spirit.

Do not wait for the open praise and worship service at church to delight yourself in the Lord. Give Him preeminence in your day. Start with thanksgiving and praise to the King of kings and Lord of lords. Keep your heart pliable. He is the potter, and we are the clay. May our prayer be "Mold me and make me after Thy will, while I am waiting, yielded and still."[3]

There Is Healing in His Presence

In the place of solitude and quietness, you learn to trust God as Father in the truest meaning of the word. He chose you before the foundation of the world. He knew the paths you would take in this earth journey. He knew your past, your present and your future. He knew the family into which you were born, the generations that have gone before and the generations that are yet to follow.

He causes everything to accommodate itself and contribute to its own end and His own purpose (Prov. 16:4)—even those things that wounded and crippled you emotionally.

In the presence of our God, there is healing. He provided for your salvation, and you are complete in Him. The healing and salvation of your soul is a process. But there comes a day when you move out of the land of hurt and lack into the land of glorious liberty.

Developing the habit of thanksgiving—an attitude of gratitude—is a very significant key in the kingdom of light. You can live in the land of the living!

The following is a prayer that God gave me one day when I was struggling to express my thanksgiving and praise:

Dear Father,

Thank You for hearing me. You see the frustration of my soul. Thank You for sending the Holy Spirit to be my Comforter and Friend in time of need. In obedience to Your Word, I choose to make a joyful noise to You and serve You with gladness. In spite sorrowful feelings, I come before Your presence with singing. I know that You are God. You made me. I am Yours and a sheep of Your pasture.

By Your grace I enter into Your gates and present an offering of thanks. Thank You for the blood of Jesus that makes it possible for me to enter into Your courts with praise regardless of my emotional distress. In the face of hurt and disappointment, I am thankful and say so. I bless and affectionately praise Your name. For You are good, and Your mercy and lovingkindness are everlasting. Your faithfulness and truth endure to all generations, and that includes my children and their children.

Thank You for my parents and my siblings. Thank You for victories and achievements in spite of the wounds and crippled emotions. My soul was bruised, and the abuses boxed me in when I was a child. You are using them for good, and I will strengthen my brothers and sisters—offering to them the comfort You have given me.

Thank You for those who deserted and betrayed me. In my vulnerable times, You took me up and You gave me rest. Thank You for Your grace that is teaching me to trust myself to hear Your voice and receive my healing. Thank You for the survival techniques that enabled me to stay alive rather than die. Thank You for life. Your life has lighted my pathway.

Oh, Father, thanks for bringing me into the land of the living! With all that is within me, I offer thanks and praise and worship You. You are my Father. Thank You for loving me with an unconditional love. Thank You for restoring my soul. In the name of Jesus.

Receive your healing and pass it on to those for whom you are praying. Determine your identity, your influence and your integrity. You are a chosen one, called to be an agent of prayer by the will of God. Your prayers will avail much, and God will reward you mightily!

Practice the presence of our Lord and maintain an attitude of gratitude. That will be your most important task in preparing for intercession. You will then be equipped to stand in the gap for others as you enter into spiritual combat unafraid.

CHAPTER 9

Praying for a Loved One

When I first began to pray for our son's deliverance from the drug scene, I had little understanding about offering up prayers of intercession, so I applied the rules governing the prayer of faith to this form of prayer. I had heard that if I prayed more than once for anything, I was praying in doubt and unbelief. However, the Holy Spirit called me to pray for David again and again.

Sometimes it seems that a mother's natural love can turn into resentment, weariness and unforgiveness. But God's love is able to sustain her, and by His grace she forgives and lets go of hurt. Her emotions run the gamut from feelings of intense love to feelings of overwhelming acrimony. Sometimes her prayers are objective; other times they are filled with fervent, passionate longing to see that child cleansed by the blood of Jesus.

When praying for a loved one, it is imperative that you admit to yourself and the Father the emotional hurts, disappointments, fears and anger that so often have been denied. Denied emotions become controllers and hinder answered prayer.

There were times when circumstances looked good, and I would relax my intercession for David, only to have to go back and pray him out of adverse circumstances again. In moments of anger, I declared that I would never pray for him again, only to find myself drawn once more by the Holy Spirit to a place of spiritual warfare or travail.

Such intense intercession is a time for speaking truly and living truly—casting down imaginations and lofty things that seek to exalt themselves above the knowledge of God.

The Long-Term Prayer Assignment

One morning while I was praying, I had a vision of a hedgerow made up of people and angels with flaming swords surrounding our son. This was most comforting to me because I theorized that the prayer assignment was complete. However, much to my dismay, David returned to the strange, bleak world of drugs and alcohol.

Then the Holy Spirit revealed that the vision was to confirm what He had spoken to my heart: *If you will pray for David's friends, I will raise up intercessors to pray for him.* He assured me that God had and that I was not alone. Not only were they praying, but also God had commissioned ministering spirits to keep David from destroying himself.

Later, David shared how God had delivered him in the face of dreadful situations.

The Father began to teach me the importance of travailing in birth again until Christ be formed in the young Christian. He revealed to me how an addictive personality can continually bounce back and forth from compulsive behaviors to freedom until he receives emotional wholeness, enabling him to overcome the toxic addiction. These addictions are symptoms of confusion, internal conflicts and crippled emotions.

The prayers of the believers would keep David until Jesus could be formed in him. His wrong thought patterns about God, about his parents and about himself were gateways that Satan used to trap him. These were rooted in emotional pain from the past, unresolved issues and unacknowledged anger.

In this type of situation, your prayer responsibility is to pull down the strongholds holding the person in bondage. In the name of Jesus, you destroy the pride that has veiled the prisoner's eyes. He is now faced with a clear decision for or against deliverance and salvation. The light of the gospel has pierced the darkness.

One day as I was reading in the Old Testament, I saw how one man refused to leave where he was to go into enemy territory. While Nehemiah was working on the wall, his enemies gathered together, calling him to come down to the plain of Ono and reason with them. But he refused, saying, "I am doing a great work, so I can't come down." Nehemiah made a decision to remain in a safe place—behind the wall.

However, David's reaction to his tempters was different; he allowed himself to be persuaded by their coaxing. Our prayers didn't override David's free will. But whenever he would go down to the enemy territory, the prayers of the saints drew him back within the hedge again.

You see, you cannot control the will of another person. Instead, you pull down the strongholds that prevent him from hearing and receiving the gospel. Sometimes he has to hear it again and again and again before the light of the truth shines in his heart. After a time, he will no longer filter the gospel through the wrong mind-sets and wrong attitudes.

So during and even after your prayer times, continue to send forth the Word of God into your loved one's life, for strongholds must be pulled down. This is a process that usually doesn't take place overnight; sometimes it's progressive. Nevertheless, people with addictive behaviors are not too hard for God.

The words you speak are creative and will not return to God void. Therefore, never be moved by good or bad circumstances; just keep your anchor firmly grounded in the Word of God. Remain steady regardless of the situation.

Examine yourself periodically. Uproot any exasperation, resentment, rancor or anger lest it produces bitterness. Forgive your loved one, and purpose to stand in the gap before God on his or her behalf. Mercy triumphs over judgment.

You don't have to fight, claw the air and scream at the devil. Submit to God and resist the devil. Then having done all to stand, stand. Stand before God reminding Him of His promises to you. You and your household shall be saved! It is a promise!

Don't abort the God-given mission. You will know through the witness of the Holy Spirit when you have fulfilled your specific assignment for a particular loved one. There will be a definite release within you—a knowing that must be experienced personally in order to be completely understood. Keep praying—extending forgiveness, obtaining mercy and grace—until the work is accomplished.

It seems to me, however, that praying for loved ones is a perpetual prayer assignment.

A Temporary Burden for Prayer

Our family was returning from a trip to see our grandparents. During the last leg of the journey, we faced what appeared to be certain death.

It was early morning, and the light of day hadn't yet appeared. No one heard the whistle of the approaching train, and my father drove across the railroad tracks. The train was upon us, but at the last possible moment my dad floor-boarded the gas pedal.

My parents and I could hardly believe we had made it. The younger children roused momentarily as we breathed a sigh of relief and praised God for doing what had looked impossible. He had saved us from disaster and kept our family alive and well. (The conductor must have been even more frightened than we were. He saw us before we saw him.)

The next morning, one of our church members called my dad to inquire if our lives had been in danger at a certain time. He said that he had woken up, looked at the clock and our faces had flashed before him. Knowing that this was an emergency prayer need, he began to pray as the Holy Spirit gave him utterance, calling for the protection of God to cover us.

Praise God! The Lord found someone who would respond to this call. This gentleman fulfilled his role as intercessor on behalf of his pastor and family in a time of crisis.

God wants your prayer time devoted to situations outside your own personal problems. Develop the mind of Christ within you; hold the thoughts, feelings and purposes of His heart.

Broaden Your Vision

The Holy Spirit desires to broaden the scope of your prayer life. Our Father has a plan for mankind, and He desires that you become involved in that plan. By the grace of God, your prayer borders are expanded beyond the confines of your home and your local church. (However, do not neglect these vital areas of prayer.)

In Psalm 2:8, the Father said: **Ask of me, and I shall give thee the heathen for thine inheritance, and the uttermost parts of the earth for thy possession.** Meditating on this passage of Scripture will broaden your vision.

The Lord imprints His intercession on the tablets of your heart, delegating prayer assignments to you as He wills. As you practice prayer, your mind is transformed. No longer consumed with temporal concerns, you become kingdom-minded in preparation for the return of Jesus. Your prayers are peppered with eternal proceedings and less with circumstantial conditions. Your level of faith increases to a level that allows you to include God's love for the nations. You begin to go beyond the needs of your family and the prayer situations of your local church.

Pray for the will of God to be done on earth as it is in heaven. Problems should not dictate your prayer life. Be led by the Spirit of God, carrying out *His* prayer assignments. Whether it is for the family, the church, the community or the nation, remain faithful to your assigned prayer burden until it is fulfilled.

Agreeing With the Plans
and Purposes of God

Make yourself available to the Holy Spirit, and get involved in the things Jesus is doing. You were destined from the beginning to be molded into His image. (Rom. 8:29.)

Act like Jesus. Walk like Jesus. Talk like Jesus. Adopt the same attitude and purpose that was in Christ Jesus. In His present-day ministry, Jesus is the High Priest who intercedes before the Father: **Seeing then that we have a great high priest, that is passed into the heavens, Jesus the Son of God, let us hold fast our profession** (Heb. 4:14).

In Greek, the word translated *profession* is *homologia,* meaning "confession."[1] Let us meet the terms of confession to God by affirming our faith in Him and His Word. This requires agreement with the plans and purposes of God.

Hebrews 4:15 says,

> **For we have not an high priest which cannot be touched with the feeling of our infirmities; but was in all points tempted like as we are, yet without sin.**

As new covenant believers, we are part of an holy priesthood (offering up spiritual sacrifices, acceptable to God by Jesus Christ), and a royal priesthood (that we should show forth the praises of Him who has called us out of darkness into His marvelous light). (1 Pet. 2:5,9.) The first ministry of a New Testament priest is to offer up praises to God; the second is to declare his wonderful salvation through a life that emulates Jesus.

Your transformed life is a testimony to your family and friends that it is possible to change. You are a living epistle, read of all men. Your life gives hope where there is no hope because it is Christ who lives in you, the hope of glory.

Assuming our positions as priests of the new covenant, we pray here on earth, and our High Priest presents our petitions before the Father. As priests, we make intercession for those who cannot or will not pray for themselves.

A Successful Prayer Life

Examination of the lives of prominent Christian men and women reveals that they were—and are—men and women of prayer. Jesus has given believers a pattern for successful living that includes a successful prayer life.

In the Song of Solomon 2:13-14, a superb passage of Scripture calls us into an intimate relationship to our Lord. The bridegroom (representing Christ) says to his beloved bride:

> **Arise, my love, my fair one, and come away. O my dove, that art in the clefts of the rock, in the secret places of the stairs, let me see thy countenance, let me hear thy voice; for sweet is thy voice, and thy countenance is comely.**

This is the call of Jesus to the church today. Everyone who spends time with Jesus discovers divine plans and purposes for his life: **The Lord confides in those who fear him; he makes his covenant known to them** (Ps. 25:14 NIV).

What has God placed on your heart? Has he called you to be the intercessor for your family? Be faithful to fulfill this call. The Christian's prayer armor is of the spirit, and God has written certain prayer ventures on the invisible breastplate of righteousness.

To be a successful intercessor, you must look beyond situations, problems and circumstances. Ask God to give you *His* burden. Jesus said, **My yoke is easy, and my burden is light** (Matt. 11:30).

CHAPTER 10

What Is Spiritual Warfare?

Prayer has the power to invoke the blessings of God, thwart the onslaughts of Satan, prevent judgment, release provision, resist temptation and enlist angelic assistance.

Prayers from the lips of earth's most ordinary Christian can stop hell's most insistent attack and command heaven's immediate response. As enforcers of Christ's victory, believers who pray will encounter many instances of spiritual warfare against enemy forces.

Dimensions of Spiritual Warfare

What is spiritual warfare? How does one engage in it? Are we to spend hours addressing the devil and his cohorts? The answers to these questions are found in the life and teaching of Jesus as He dealt with the devil and taught His disciples how to do so.

In Luke 10, Jesus sent His disciples out to teach and preach the gospel of the kingdom. When He did, He gave them the power, right and authority to tread on serpents, scorpions and over all over the power of the enemy. (v. 19.)

When the disciples returned to joyfully report that even demons were subject to them in His name, Jesus quickly redirected their focus, emphasizing that their names were written in heaven (which afforded them authority) instead of the fact that they had authority over an already defeated foe. (v. 20.)

So what is spiritual warfare? Simply put, spiritual warfare is the prayer or action that addresses and defies Satan and enforces his defeat from a position of victory through the authority and victory of Jesus Christ.

Jesus wasted little time conversing with the devil. He simply declared, "It is written…" And we cannot attempt to overcome the devil with a long, entangled dialogue.

We overcome the devil by the blood of the Lamb and by the Word of God in our testimony. (Rev. 12:11.) This is not, however, our only spiritual weapon to enforce the victory of Jesus Christ. Another weapon of warfare for us as overcomers is the refusal to love our lives so much that we are afraid of death.

Do not discount demons and their abilities. Demons are real, and they are real adversaries. They cannot arbitrarily overpower anyone; they must be given access in order to lead astray and deceive:

> **If the Good News we preach is veiled from anyone, it is a sign that they are perishing. Satan, the god of this evil world, has blinded the minds of those who don't believe.**
>
> **2 Corinthians 4:3,4 NLT**

Jesus warned us about giving too much attention to demonic spirits. He said we are to rejoice not because the demons are subject to us but because our names are written in heaven. We are to set our minds on things that are eternal so we can be well-balanced and enduring.

It is imperative that we learn how to pray effectively for the lost and for believers who are struggling in the midst of trials, tribulations and temptations. Fortunately, the weapons of our warfare are not carnal but mighty through God to the pulling down of strongholds. (2 Cor. 10:4.) We will look at this passage of Scripture later in this chapter.

When the seventy returned to Jesus in Luke 10:17, they were thrilled that the demons were subject to them. They said to Jesus, **"Even the demons danced to your tune!"** (Luke 10:17 THE MESSAGE).

Jesus answered,

"I know. I saw Satan fall, a bolt of lightning out of the sky. See what I've given you? Safe passage as you walk on snakes and scorpions, and protection from every assault of the Enemy. No one can put a hand on you. All the same, the great triumph is not in your authority over evil, but in God's authority over you and presence with you. Not what you do for God but what God does for you—that's the agenda for rejoicing."

Luke 10:18-20, THE MESSAGE

Jesus redirected their focus.

Word-Centered Spiritual Warfare

Peter instructs us to

Be well balanced (temperate, sober of mind), be vigilant and cautious at all times, for that enemy of yours, the devil, roams around like a lion roaring [in fierce hunger], seeking someone to seize upon and devour.

1 Peter 5:8 AMP

When we first discover we have power over the enemy, we are sometimes tempted to get out of control. In order to stay well-balanced, we must keep ourselves Word-centered.

You may be surrounded by spiritual warfare, but you don't have to live in a constant state of conflict. However, if you follow the prayer lives of some, you might think the devil is omnipresent, which is not true. Every cough and personal discomfort is attributed to him, and he is addressed promptly in firm tones with "Get away! Stop it! Leave me alone!"

I have observed the fruit of this form of spiritual warfare, and I don't believe it works. Furthermore, I find no basis for it in the Word of God or in the example of Jesus' dealing with the devil.

These believers who appear to "practice the presence" of Satan are constantly reminding themselves and everyone in earshot that the devil is harassing them. Every time you talk with them they are "fighting the good fight of faith," meaning, "I'm sick or I'm having a difficult time." They would rather cuss than make a "bad confession." They pray with a great vengeance and are constantly warring against evil spirits.

On occasion, I have had the opportunity to speak with these precious people. I believe they do love God, but I find talking with them very frustrating. Their unhealed hurts, unmet needs and unresolved issues are evident, but they refuse any reasoning that contradicts their religious mind-set.

I discovered that my discussion with them resulted in disappointment for me and reinforced their doctrines. Today, rather than attempt to reason with them, I pray for God to open the eyes of their understanding, and pull down, crush and demolish every stronghold that would keep them from the knowledge of God.

Rather than admitting hurt and uncovering the roots of their anger, they unleash vehement outbursts on Satan and sometimes castigate loved ones. It is not unusual to see them thrown into a state of panic in any given set of circumstances, although they would never admit it.

When someone pushes their buttons, their reaction is controlled by a belief that a demonic spirit is motivating the individual to take advantage of them and abuse them verbally or emotionally. They don't care who is listening; the devil is not going to dupe them.

I've watched people actually run away from these Christians or at least attempt to ignore them, but their reaction is "I don't care what they think. The devil is not getting away with this."

Believers who attribute too much ability to the devil view every event—no matter how small or large—as either caused by God or the devil. It never occurs to them that their personal choices determine their destiny. Even though they may ask God, "Show me to me," when He reveals an issue He wants them to face, they rebuke the devil.

I've noticed that these demon fighters seldom examine themselves to expose their own wrong thought patterns, attitudes and motives, but they are quick to see the faults or "demonic activity" in others. They constantly wage war against an already defeated foe, thus empowering him to ruffle their feathers.

Such erroneous thoughts about spiritual warfare do not correspond with the Word of God. In the Old Testament, God's people lifted up praise as their only weapon in battle after the Lord said, **Be not afraid nor dismayed by reason of this great multitude; for the battle is not yours, but God's** (2 Chron. 20:15).

If the battle is not ours, why are some believers fighting and screaming at unseen forces? Spiritual warfare is real, but God's idea of the battle is different from ours. And His methods of "fighting" it are very different from our own.

A Worthwhile Fight

The Jews and the Romans celebrated their victories by triumphal processions. Glorious parades were a sign of a victorious battle.

For example, Miriam led women and children in a procession with tambourine, musical instruments, songs and dancing after the defeat of Pharaoh's army. The horse and the rider were thrown into the sea! (Ex. 15:1-21.)

Another woman, Deborah, sang a hymn of triumphant after the destruction of an enemy who tormented and abused women. (Judg. 5:1-31.)

When our Lord faced the devil, He stripped him of authority and made an open display of him. A triumphant conqueror leads a triumphant people, who are the administrators of His triumphant victory the enforcers of the victory won at Calvary.

Paul describes the kind of "fight" believers are to engage in: it is the fight of faith which activates our covenant as we take our triumphant position in Christ by proclaiming the knowledge of His victory for all who believe: **But thanks be to God, who always leads us in triumphal procession in**

Christ and through us spreads everywhere the fragrance of the knowledge of him (2 Cor. 2:14 NIV).

Jesus is the victor and worthy of our praise. So let's not concentrate on the devil, but set our minds on things that are above. Let's **fight the worthwhile battle of the faith, keep our grip on that life eternal to which you have been called, and to which you boldly professed your loyalty before many witnesses** (1 Tim. 6:12 PHILLIPS).

Paul gives instruction regarding the fight of faith in 1 Timothy 6:11-12 (WUEST). After warning Timothy of the dangers of covetousness and the love of money, Paul addressed him directly:

> **But, as for you, O man of God, these things be constantly fleeing. But be as constantly eagerly seeking to acquire righteousness, godly piety, faith divine and self-sacrificial love, steadfastness, gentleness.**
>
> **Be constantly engaging in the contest of Faith, which contest is marked by its beauty of technique. Take possession of the eternal life into a participation of which you were called and concerning which you gave testimony to your agreement with the good profession [you made] in the presence of many witnesses.**

We are to be alert, renewing our minds and pulling down every reasoning that would exalt itself above the Word of God as we run our spiritual race with patience. Notice there is no mention of fighting the devil in this Scripture. Instead, we make a decision to give the devil no place by fleeing from evil and following after righteousness, godliness, faith, love, patience and meekness. This warfare is not just words, but action. Our behavior is a statement of victory or defeat.

You cannot be passive when opposition and temptation presents itself. You have to actively persevere in faith in order to prevail over the enemy's strategies.

So how can you aggressively resist the devil? Pursue God!

Satan is a defeated foe, and his strategy is deceit. Wrong mind-sets open the door for demonic activity to continue through family lines, allowing generational curses to be passed down. Entire regions form wrong cultural ideas. These ideas become so entrenched that the devil has an open door to control and manipulate communities.

But we have the power to enforce spiritual laws and defeat the schemes of the evil one. Therefore, we should put on the whole armor of God: **Above all, taking the shield of faith, wherewith ye shall be able to quench all the fiery darts of the wicked** (Eph.6:16).

As believers, we are seated in heavenly places in Christ, who is seated at the right hand of the Father **far above all principality, and power, and might, and dominion, and every name that is named, not only in this world, but also in that which is to come** (Eph. 1:21).

Jesus Christ is the Head of all things to the church, which is His body, the fullness of Him that filleth all in all. (Eph. 1:22,23; 2:6.) We are seated above the fray. In Christ, we have authority over the enemy. Therefore, we can rejoice and *rest,* knowing it is God who gives us power, authority and lasting victory. It is not in our strength or our might; rather, it is all in the name of Jesus that we gain the victory.

Personal Spiritual Warfare

It is past time for you to face the truth about the struggle that engages you. I like what this writer has to say about it:

> You may have been going through the motions of your own Christianity without realizing that you are in a deep struggle, a struggle from which you cannot escape.

> You successfully hide your inner turmoil from others and wear an outward expression of complete consecration to God, but you keep wounds, conflicts, and sins hidden deep within.[1]

What are these struggles? Paul emphasized standing against the wiles of the devil. Both James and Peter indicated that we are to resist the devil, and he will flee from us. But the greatest warfare is the struggle between the spirit and the flesh or the soul.

The soul does not want to give up its authority to rule and reign in an individual's life. The soul clings to self-pity, self-righteousness, selfishness, self-centeredness and the judging and criticizing of others. It hangs on to its strongholds at any cost. Sometimes the cost is ill health, a mental breakdown or both.

Spiritual warfare of the saints is revealed in Ephesians 6:10-20. In this passage, Paul speaks of our struggle against principalities, against powers, against the rulers of darkness and against spiritual wickedness in high places.

The enemy looks for a wrong thought pattern, wrong attitude or wrong motive; then he shoots his fiery dart at our personal unresolved conflicts. He has to have something to inflame. He can't read or control our thoughts, but he can influence our minds if we give him place.

Regional Spiritual Warfare

Cultural mores and social customs are passed down from one generation to another. This practice opens the door for certain demonic spirits to rule over a territory. Strongholds can be established in a region by adopting worldly philosophy, religious dogmas, superstition and ideas fashioned after this world's external, superficial customs. These proud arguments are obstacles that set themselves up against the knowledge of God.

However, Paul explains to the church that we have spiritual weapons that are mighty through God to the pulling down of strongholds:

> **For though we live in the world, we do not wage war as the world does. The weapons we fight with are not the weapons of the world. On the contrary, they have divine power to demolish strongholds.**
>
> **2 Cor. 10:3,4** NIV

Recognize the Enemy

In natural warfare one must recognize the enemy. The same is true spiritually.

There was a time when I treated my husband as though he were my enemy. The children and I were in church; we hardly missed a service. But my husband had quit attending church during the years when he worked full time and attended college. During those quarters when he carried a full schedule, we seldom saw him.

Having Everette return to church with us became an obsession with me. I tried every tactic I knew to force him to go. After all, this was certainly the will of God. Didn't God say, "Forsake not the assembling of yourselves together"? (Heb. 10:25.) Also, it was Everette's duty to be a good example to our children. In addition to all this, I was tired of feeling so alone.

Every Sunday morning, the battleground was set. I woke the children, fed them breakfast and saw that they got dressed properly. Meanwhile, their dad remained in bed. At every opportunity, I ran to the bedroom either nagging, coercing, speaking gently or screaming. Sometimes I would wake the children early and send them in to wake Daddy.

One day the Holy Spirit said to me, "Since you have prayed, believe." The gentle voice of the Spirit instructed me to treat my husband just as I would if he were attending church. I realized that believing is acting as though God has heard and answered prayer. Faith is active.

So often women say, "I have prayed. Now what do I do? How do I behave toward my husband?" God always reveals the way, the truth and the life to those who diligently seek Him.

Sunday mornings were certainly easier for the children and me once I changed my manipulative behavior through the grace given me. Personal strongholds of control were uprooted as the Holy Spirit gave me the power to obey God.

My prayers were no longer desperate and demanding; I entered into a place of contentment and rest. No longer did I view my husband as an enemy. Instead, I wrestled against my own wrong thinking—and the wrestling was not exercised in screams and railings against the devil. In the midst of it all, the Holy Spirit taught me that walking in quiet confidence, peace and joy was a mighty enforcement of resistance against Satan's devices.

It was only a few weeks later on a Sunday morning that I walked into the living room and saw my husband dressed. When I asked where he was going, he announced that he thought he would go to church with us.

The Devices of Satan

Paul wrote in 2 Corinthians 2:11: **For we are not ignorant of his [Satan's] devices.** God intends for us to know and understand the tactics of the enemy. When we study the Scriptures, we learn to recognize how he thinks. This places us at a great advantage, enabling us to be on the offensive instead of the defensive. We must be aware of Satan's strategy and take a stand, resisting his attempts to devour us.

Jesus exposed Satan as a liar, the father of lies, a murderer, a thief, an adversary and a deceiver. He is the accuser of the brethren. He will attempt to overcome us by diverting our attention away from his actions. At the other extreme, he delights when we blame him for everything, diverting our attention away from seeing the truth about ourselves. We must stay well-balanced and alert, giving him no place to get a foothold in our lives.

Ephesians 6:10-18 describes our prayer armor and exposes the enemy and his ranks. In this passage, Paul exhorts believers to develop and exercise courage in spiritual warfare against the demonic enemies of God.

These unseen enemies attach themselves to our wrong thought patterns, attitudes, motives and behaviors. Although they can't read our minds, they look for areas of unhealed hurts, unmet needs and unresolved issues, using these vulnerable places to reinforce our wrong thought patterns until they become a stronghold.

Satan tries to turn us from God—to create fear, doubt and unbelief and to induce us to be unfaithful to God's Word. Using deceit, pressure and cunning craftiness as snares intended to keep us focused on problems, the devil provokes us to believe we are victims or to be aggressive in our language and behavior. His tactic is to keep us off balance.

Satan also sends us thoughts of accusation against people in an attempt to create a proud look, a lying tongue, hands that shed innocent blood, a heart that devises wicked imaginations, feet that are quick to rush into evil and a false witness that speaks lies. (Prov. 6:17-19.) Our strongholds of rigidity, denial, emotional isolation, silence, unforgiveness, control, confusion, distrust or fear enable us to rationalize and justify our actions. We must always remember, however, that God has given us the power to strip off the old man and put on the new.

Satan's greatest delight is to disturb harmony, and he will use words to create great winds and waves of discord. Another one of his favorite ploys is to heap condemnation on the believer, turning him against himself. But Paul makes it clear that we are not to come against one another or ourselves— only against spiritual rebel forces.

Wrestling in the Spirit

Two important questions to ask in regard to spiritual warfare is "Who exactly are we waging war against?" and "What type of action does 'spiritual warfare' really require?" Paul gives us answers in Ephesians 6:10:12 NKJV:

> **Finally, my brethren, be strong in the Lord and in the power of His might. Put on the whole armor of God, that you may be able to stand against the wiles of the devil.**
>
> **For we do not wrestle against flesh and blood, but against principalities, against powers, against the rulers of the darkness of this age, against spiritual hosts of wickedness in the heavenly places.**

Jesus knew there would be people who would not accept us but would set themselves against the Word of God we preach. Yet still He said to us,

> **Love your enemies, bless those who curse you, do good to those who hate you, and pray for those who spitefully use you, and persecute you, that you may be the sons of your Father in heaven; for he makes His sun rise on the evil and on the good, and sends rain on the just and on the unjust.**
>
> Matthew 5:44,45 NKJV

Our Lord was never against a person—only against the evil one who holds people in bondage.

Jesus spoke out against the tactics of religious leaders whose teachings put heavy burdens on the people. He did not mince words but called them "vipers" and "whitewashed sepulchres." Yet if the religious leaders could have let go of their religious dogmas and believed that Jesus was the Son of God, maybe the story would have been different. John 3:16 says, **For God so loved *the world*, that he gave his only begotten Son.** Jesus loved His people even when they rejected Him; He longed for them and wept over Jerusalem.

Paul's writings are in harmony with the teachings of Jesus. He says we are not to set ourselves against people. But if our struggle is with Satan and not people, what is the practical application of this Scripture? How does one wrestle with the devil?

Scripture must always harmonize. If the battle is the Lord's, if Jesus gave His disciples power over demons, if He stripped principalities and made a show of them openly, why are we in a wrestling match with the devil? Could it be that our battle is in the mind—those unrenewed areas of the mind? The battle seems to be between the old man and the new.

In *Vine's Expository Dictionary*, I came across two seemingly insignificant shades of meaning for this word *wrestle*: "sway" and "vibrate." Mr. Vine wrote that "...wrestling...is used figuratively, in Ephesians 6:12, of the spiritual conflict engaged in by believers."[2]

The two synonyms given made no sense to me. I tried first one meaning in the sentence: "We *sway* not against flesh and blood"; then I tried the other: "We *vibrate* not against flesh and blood." It appeared that these two words simply did not work in that context.

When I considered the word *wrestle,* I immediately had a mental image of two massive men in various holds, each trying to pin the other for the count. *If Jesus didn't defeat Satan,* I thought, *I am in big trouble.* Somehow I could not see myself in this kind of struggle with the devil.

However, mental images of the words *sway* and *vibrate* didn't bring any acceptable revelation. I knew that Scripture must interpret Scripture. But the only swaying I could think of that might be scriptural was that of the trees planted by the rivers of living waters in Psalm 1.

Of course, this could be a representation of believers as they are buffeted by the storms and winds of life. That interpretation seemed pleasing to me. It illustrated that we could not be uprooted by the enemy's strategies when they come against us. But I knew there was more to be understood.

Webster gives us insight into the word *sway.* Among his definitions are two very appropriate meanings as they relate to the believer: "to vacillate or alternate between one position, opinion, etc. and another."[3]

I can remember the time when I was constantly being pulled back and forth between righteousness and unrighteousness. Romans 7 described my mental and emotional state of dubiousness, distrust and unbelief. Yet on the other hand, I did believe. However, a double-minded person receives nothing from God.

Then in my studies, the verb form of the word *wrestle* caught my attention, and it took on a new framework in my mind: "sovereign power or authority; rule; dominion...to *hold sway,* to reign or prevail.[4]

According to Ephesians 2:6, we believers have been raised up together and made to sit together in the heavenly places in Christ Jesus. This places **us far above all principality and power and might and dominion, and every name that is named, not only in this age but also in that which is to come** (Eph.1:19 NKJV).

To the human mind, this is too good to be true. Why is it that we are "far above"? Because we are in Christ! In that name above all names, we have been given the authority to hold sway over Satan and his forces.

A couple of other verb forms summed it all up for me: "to cause (a person, an opinion, actions, etc.) to be inclined a certain way or be turned from a given course; influence or divert [*swayed* by promises]; [Archaic] to *wield* (a scepter, etc.)"[5]

We have the promises of God and the authority, power and might to renew our minds and put action to our faith. As we wield the sword of the Spirit (the Word of God), we divert Satan, causing him to turn from a given course. It is my prayer that we will be enlightened to know the exceeding greatness of His power toward us who believe.

Isn't this what we are attempting to do in spiritual warfare—to turn the course of Satan, to divert him from that which he has plotted and planned against our families, our churches and our nations? In spiritual warfare, we enforce the victory of Jesus Christ, holding sway over the enemy, not over human beings.

When I first began meditating on this, I remembered Psalm 126:1, where it says, **When the Lord turned again the captivity of Zion, we were like them that dream.** It is almost too good to be true. We shall know the *truth*, and the *truth* shall make us free!

We must awake to righteousness. There is no place for moaning and groaning about the wiles of the devil. We are more than conquerors through Him Who loves us!

Vibrating Light or Wavering Opinion?

How can we apply the word *vibrate* to spiritual warfare? Again, we turn to the dictionary for a detailed definition. *Vibrate* means "to give off (light or sound) by vibration."[6]

Vibration is also "an emotional quality or supernatural emanation that is sensed by another person or thing."[7]

When you walk into a room, you can often sense the peace or the tension released in the atmosphere. You may even become very uncomfortable if you cannot identify a cause for the "vibes" surrounding you. The pressure begins and increases, causing you to want to run away or hide. No one is giving you a clue of the situation, but you sense sensations of unspoken agitation emanating from those present. Amazingly, the presence of another person who comes into the room can release peaceful vibrations, dispelling the unrest.

Havoc must take place in the seat of Satan's empire as we believers stand clothed in the armor of light, praying all manner of prayer. Light dispels darkness: **And the Light shines on in the darkness, for the darkness has never overpowered it [put it out or absorbed it or appropriated it, and is unreceptive to it]** (John 1:5 AMP).

Jesus said to His disciples, **You are the light of the world. A city that is set on a hill cannot be hidden** (Matt. 5:14 NKJV). Paul wrote, **For you were once darkness, but now you are light in the Lord. Walk as children of light** (Eph. 5:8 NKJV).

Another meaning of the word *vibrate* is "to waver or vacillate, as between two choices."[8] There are times when we stagger between belief and doubt, faith and fear. This frustrates the purposes and plans of spiritual warfare. Swaying or vacillating between two opinions is the result of the presence of strongholds that have not yet been pulled down. But remember, **the weapons of our warfare are not carnal, but mighty through God to the pulling down of strong holds** (2 Cor. 10:4). It is possible to overcome doubt and fear when we stagger not at the promises of God. (Rom. 4:20.)

How do we wrestle against these spiritual rebels that are loose in the world today? We put on the whole armor of God and pray scriptural prayers **at all times (on every occasion, in every season) in the Spirit, with all [manner of] prayer and entreaty** (Eph. 6:18 AMP). We speak God's Word, praying with our understanding.

Jesus declared, "It is written;" therefore, we declare, "It is written." God's Word is our sword, and when the enemy comes to destroy our homes, our health, our churches and our communities, we remind him of his defeat by affirming God's Word over everything that concerns us.

The entrance of God's Word brings light, dispelling darkness. (Ps. 119:130.) So turn to the Word for answers. Affirm the Word in your meditation and through prayer. There is no better prayer book. God is watching over His Word to perform it. (Jer. 1:12.)

Having Done All

We are in a fight to the finish with a predetermined outcome. The battle is the Lord's, and the victory is ours. Our responsibility is to *stand*, and having done all to stand—STAND. I like Eugene H. Peterson's interpretation of Ephesians 6:10-19 (THE MESSAGE):

> **And that about wraps it up. God is strong, and he wants you strong. So take everything the Master has set out for you, well-made weapons of the best materials. And put them to use so you will be able to stand up to everything the Devil throws your way. This is no afternoon athletic contest that we'll walk away from and forget about in a couple of hours. This is for keeps, a life-or-death fight to the finish against the Devil and all his angels.**
>
> **Be prepared. You're up against far more than you can handle on your own. Take all the help you can get, every weapon God has issued, so that when it's all over but the shouting you'll still be on your feet. Truth, righteousness, peace, faith, and salvation are more than words. Learn how to apply them. You'll need them throughout your life. God's Word is an indispensable weapon. In the same way, prayer is essential in this ongoing warfare. Pray hard and long. Pray for your brothers and sisters. Keep your eyes open. Keep each other's spirits up so that no one falls behind or drops out.**

**And don't forget to pray for me. Pray that I'll know what to
say and have the courage to say it at the right time, telling the
mystery to one and all, the Message that I, jailbird preacher that
I am, am responsible for getting out.**

A spiritual war is being waged against the body of Christ—a war
between righteousness and unrighteousness. In a wrestling match, the
contenders have to remain well-balanced, alert, attentive and vigilant.
Unseen forces are competing for our faith. Satan is a defeated foe, but his
tactics are not nonsensical and meaningless. His devises are subtle.

Paul uses the term *wrestle* metaphorically to define the life-and-death
situation that attempts to destroy our stand. In our culture, this term is not
as imposing as it was at the time it was written.

> When we consider that the loser in a Greek wrestling contest had his eyes
> gouged out with resulting blindness for the rest of his days, we can form some
> conception of the Ephesian Greek's reaction to Paul's illustration. The Christian's
> wrestling against the powers of darkness is no less desperate and fateful.[9]

Immediately, Paul draws our attention to a heavily armed soldier. Each
of us as individuals has to dress him- or herself in the whole armor provided
by God. This armor has been tested and tried, and we know it is impenetrable as we do everything to stand and then *stand*, clothed in the armor.

We put on the belt of truth and the breastplate of righteousness. We
take up the shield of faith, deflecting every fiery dart, and wield the sword
of the Spirit, enforcing the triumphant victory of our Lord Jesus Christ. At
all times we wear the helmet of salvation and keep our feet shod in the
preparation of the gospel of peace.

How do we stand? First, obedience to God's Word is essential. Throughout the Scriptures, we discover how to stand as soldiers of the Cross: **Stand
fast therefore in the liberty by which Christ has made us free, and do not
be entangled again with a yoke of bondage** (Gal. 5:1 NKJV). We must be
vigilant and maintain the truth that set us free by declaring the Word of
truth and walking in the truth.

Second, we must be strong in the grace that is in Christ Jesus and **endure hardship as a good soldier of Jesus Christ. No one engaged in warfare entangles himself with the affairs of this life, that he may please him who enlisted him as a soldier** (2 Tim. 2:3-4 NKJV).

Often people wonder, *What do I do now? I have done all I know to do, prayed all that I know to pray. What does it mean to stand?* One of the meanings of the Greek word for *stand* is to abide. Jesus said, **If you live in Me [abide vitally united to Me] and My words remain in you and continue to live in your hearts, ask whatever you will, and it shall be done for you** (John 15:7 AMP).

As you stand, do not neglect the disciplines of prayer and Bible study.

> **Pay attention, my child, to what I say. Listen carefully. Don't lose sight of my words. Let them penetrate deep within your heart, for they bring life and radiant health to anyone who discovers their meaning.**
>
> **Above all else, guard your heart, for it affects everything you do. Avoid all perverse talk; stay far from corrupt speech. Look straight ahead, and fix your eyes on what lies before you. Mark out a straight path for your feet; then stick to the path and stay safe. Don't get sidetracked; keep your feet from following evil.**
>
>

Proverbs 4:20-27 NLT

Stagger not at the promises of God. Do not faint or grow weary as some do. As Galatians 6:9 (NKJV) says, **And let us not grow weary while doing good, for in due season we shall reap if we do not lose heart.** I like Wuest's comment:

> The historian, Gibbon, relates how the relaxation of discipline and the disuse of exercise rendered soldiers less willing and less able to support the fatigue of the service. They complained of the weight of their armor, and obtained permission to lay aside their cuirasses and helmets.[10]

There is spiritual warfare in the very atmosphere, but you are no longer children of disobedience—you are not a victim. You have the God-given ability to withstand, stand against, resist and oppose the onslaught of demonic forces.

Trust the Holy Spirit to lead and direct you in your prayer journey. Having done all to stand, rejoice in the promises of God and praise Him. Wait on Him. Complete your stand to its ultimate victorious conclusion. Our God reigns!

In Christ we are more than conquerors! Jesus said, **These things I have spoken to you, that in Me you may have peace. In the world you will have tribulation; but be of good cheer, I have overcome the world** (John 16:33 NKJV). This same Jesus said for us to watch and pray that we enter not into temptation. Today we have the victory: **This is the victory that has overcome the world—our faith** (1 John 5:4 NKJV).

There will be those times when the enemy shoots his fiery darts, attempting to deceive you as he did Eve by asking, "Has not God said...?" (Gen. 3:10.) Or he may use other angles, such as thoughts of doubt, unbelief and distrust. To the minister he may ask, "Who do you think you are? Your children are proving that your prayers do not work. How can you possibly think that you have anything to offer the people?"

But don't give place to the devil. Withstand him, firm in the faith.

When you are tempted to give up, remember:

> **How can you say the Lord does not see your troubles? How can you say God refuses to hear your case? Have you never heard or understood? Don't you know that the Lord is the everlasting God, the Creator of all the earth? He never grows faint or weary. No one can measure the depths of his understanding.**
>
> **He gives power to those who are tired and worn out; he offers strength to the weak. Even youths will become exhausted, and young men will give up. But those who wait on the Lord will find new strength. They will fly high on wings like eagles. They will run and not grow weary. They will walk and not faint.**
>
> **Isaiah 40:27-31** NLT

The Rewards of Standing

God's promises to Joshua are as real today as they were when He spoke them:

> **No one will be able to stand up against you all the days of your life. As I was with Moses, so I will be with you; I will never leave you nor forsake you.**
>
> **Joshua 1:5** NIV

When you place your faith in the promises of God, others will not be able to stand against you. We know that Moses and Joshua both knew God. They talked with Him, and He talked with them. Prayer was a lifestyle, not a ritual. These Old Testament characters were obedient and abided in the presence of God.

In Deuteronomy are listed the blessings for obedience and the curses for disobedience:

> **If you fully obey the Lord your God by keeping all the commands I am giving you today, the Lord your God will exalt you above all the nations of the world. You will experience all these blessings if you obey the Lord your God.**
>
> **The Lord will conquer your enemies when they attack you. They will attack you from one direction, but they will scatter from you in seven!**
>
> **Deuteronomy 28:1,2,7** NLT

In 2 Samuel 23 is a listing of King David's mightiest men and their exploits. One of them was Shammah son of Agee from Harar. The Philistines gathered at Lehi and attacked Israel. The Bible reveals the stand of this lone soldier against the Philistines after the Israelite army fled: **But Shannah held his ground in the middle of the field and beat back the Philistines. So the Lord brought about a great victory** (2 Sam. 23:12).

There will be those times when you have to wield the sword of the Spirit, defeating the lies of the enemy. Do not give in to his tactics. Speak to the mountain of doubt and unbelief. Replace reasonings and "stinking thinking" with God-thoughts. Pull down any stronghold that would give the devil place, bringing all your thoughts into obedience to the Lord Jesus Christ. God will not fail one word of His promise. The victory is yours!

Praise Wins the Victory

When you are standing on the promises of God, your **faith is the substance of things hoped for, the evidence of things not seen** (Heb. 11:1). What can you do during this period of waiting for the manifestation of things not yet seen? Each morning and evening, stand before the Lord to sing songs of thanks and praise to Him. (1 Chron. 23:30.) Praise drives back the enemy.

Second Chronicles 20 illustrates this biblical truth. It is the account of the time Jehoshaphat heard that Moab, Ammon and Edom, who had declared war on him, were on their way. Jehoshaphat was alarmed and sought the Lord for guidance.

The king stood before the people of Judah and Jerusalem in front of the new courtyard at the temple of the Lord and prayed: "Whenever we are faced with any calamity such as war, disease or famine, we can come to stand in Your presence before the temple where Your name is honored. We can cry out to You to save us, and You will hear us and rescue us." Jehoshaphat was not afraid to declare His confidence in Jehovah before the congregation, and God gave them a plan.

Through His prophet, the Lord said, "Listen, King Jehoshaphat! Listen, all you people of Judah and Jerusalem! This is what the Lord says: Do not be afraid! Don't be discouraged by this mighty army, for the battle is not yours, but God's. You will not even need to fight. Take your positions; then stand still and watch the Lord's victory. Go out there tomorrow, for the Lord is with you!"

After consulting the leaders of the people, the king appointed singers to walk ahead of the army, singing to the Lord and praising Him for His holy splendor. They sang, "Give thanks to the Lord; his faithful love endures forever!"

When Israel approached the battle scene, they discovered dead men and found vast amounts of equipment, clothing and other valuables—more than they could carry. There was so much plunder, it took them three days just to collect it all! They stood before God and waited on His plan, and when He gave them instruction, they obeyed, giving praise to their God.

The battle belongs to the Lord. Stand and see the salvation of God!

Take Your Stand on Solid Ground

Having done all to stand, we are to stand. But we do not stand in our own strength. These Old Testament individuals were human beings, yet they were able to stand before the Lord. How could they stand in the presence of God? Because God makes His people's feet like the feet of a deer and enables them to stand on the heights! (Ps. 18:33.)

A question is asked in Psalm 24 that we must ask ourselves:

> **Who shall ascend into the hill of the Lord? or who shall stand in his holy place? He that hath clean hands, and a pure heart; who hath not lifted up his soul unto vanity, nor sworn deceitfully.**
>
> **Psalm 24:3**

Your stand must be taken on solid, firm, unmovable ground. The Lord has placed you there: **He lifted me out of the slimy pit, out of the mud and mire; he set my feet on a rock and gave me a firm place to stand** (Ps. 40:2 NIV).

God is not a man that He should lie. Psalm 33:11 promises that **the plans of the Lord stand firm forever, the purposes of his heart through all generations.**

Storm clouds may gather in life, bringing tests and trials our way. But when the storm has swept by and the dust has settled, we who are righteous in Christ remain standing firm forever! (Prov. 10:25.)

CHAPTER 11

Prayer Group Guidelines

Organization is necessary when two or more people join together to complete any task. A prayer project is no different.

Jesus said, **For where two or three gather together because they are mine, I am there among them** (Matt. 18:20 NLT). In a group setting, our first course of action is to acknowledge His leadership and to realize that He is among us to help us develop and maintain the unity that assures us of answered prayer.

After we acknowledge the leadership of Jesus in our prayer group, we must then recognize a leader for the group who is submitted to Christ's leadership—a leader who "manages things" yet gently leads people without coercion.

Steps to Organization

Good organization creates structure to accommodate the direction and move of the Spirit of God in prayer. The first steps to establishing order are to determine the guidelines of operation and the purpose or focus of prayer.

Guidelines give us purpose and direction. A *guideline* is defined as "a standard or principle by which to make a judgment or determine a policy or course of action."[1]

One group that I taught and led in prayer was called the Acts 2:42 Fellowship Group. This Scripture was our guideline; it kept us on the course we believed God had assigned to us.

Guidelines for the Pastor
or Ministry Director

The relationship of the pastor or ministry director to the prayer group is of utmost importance. It was my privilege at one time to pastor a church. During that time, God graciously revealed to me a pastor's responsibilities toward a prayer group.

As pastor, I felt that God wanted me to be the prayer group leader rather than to appoint someone. This gave me an opportunity to interact with a faithful group of prayer warriors who were of one mind and heart. However, as president of Word Ministries, I was led to appoint a prayer coordinator to be responsible to train others as prayer leaders.

The guidelines we established proved effective for unifying the prayer groups. The prayer coordinator and I met each week. I also periodically met with the other leaders and their respective groups.

As pastor or ministry director, we must intimately know God by precept and practice in order to effectively teach and train others in the area of prayer. We must attend to the study of God's Word and develop a lifestyle of prayer. In other words, we must practice what we preach.

Organizing prayer groups can be both frustrating and rewarding. It's a serious proposition to endorse and promote united prayer—one that requires skill, wise counsel and instruction so the responsible parties will be able to steer their course rightly.

We have witnessed the unfortunate results of prayer groups left to their own devices without instruction from the pastor. The wise leader gives godly instruction.

> **Give instruction to a wise man and he will be yet wiser; teach
> a righteous man (one upright and in right standing with God)
> and he will increase in learning.**
>
> **Proverbs 9:9** AMP

How To Achieve Unity of Purpose

The pastor or ministry leader has an obligation to teach and train those who are willing to serve behind the scenes as agents of intercessory prayer. After a time of prayer, the Lord gave me the following guidelines for pastors to help them achieve unity within the prayer groups of the church:

1. Follow the revealed plan of God by effectively communicating that plan to those who pray for the church or ministry. (Well-meaning people who are seeking "their ministries" may interject an alternate vision that is meritorious or even excellent, but not God's plan for your ministry. Don't be drawn away by such distractions and thus delay the work of God.)

2. Choose a prayer leader who is of good reputation, full of the Holy Ghost and wisdom and skilled in the Word of righteousness. First Thessalonians 5:12 (AMP) says, **Now also we beseech you, brethren, get to know those who labor among you [recognize them for what they are].**

3. Maintain open communication with the prayer leader, and be willing to listen with open heart and mind.

4. Set aside time to pray with the prayer group and to express your appreciation to its members for faithfully serving as a hidden arm of the ministry. Give honor where honor is due.

5. Give the prayer group leader a statement of beliefs, a copy of the vision and a definite job description. The group leader needs to have a clear understanding of what is expected of him.

6. Establish the leader by delegating the authority he needs to fulfill the assigned mission.

The effectiveness of your public ministry is a direct reflection of your prayer life. Your study time is the highest form of worship, and your prayer life is an expression of the power that is at work in you. Jesus is our example, and prayer was His key focus.

Jesus prayed alone on many occasions, and the heavens were opened. However, He desired and sought prayer support, as evidenced by His request that His disciples watch and pray with Him during His time of testing in the Garden of Gethsemane.

If the Lord Jesus needed prayer support in His trials, then it seems obvious that those of us in the ministry today must develop and rely on the kind of prayerful aid and support that other concerned believers can provide.

Designate a Leader

The thoughts and guidelines I am sharing in this chapter have been collected over years of experience as an intercessory prayer group leader, as a leader of a teaching and prayer ministry and as a pastor.

Through the years, I have found that it is essential that a prayer group designate a leader. I have also found that constantly submitting to God's ways and seeking His wisdom and understanding are the key ingredients for leading a group.

A prayer group without a designated leader seldom survives. Groups need someone who will keep the focus and harmony of the group stable and on course. Leaderless groups who spiritualize to the point of ignoring practical obligations, such as job and family responsibilities, tread on dangerous ground and soon dissolve.

An effective prayer group leader maintains the balance between the practical and the spiritual aspects of guiding intercessory efforts in prayer. The leader should continually seek God's guidance for the prayer group and pray for each team player individually.

How a Leader's Personality
Shapes the Prayer Group

If you are a prayer group leader, an understanding of personality differences will give you the needed insight to promote harmony within the prayer group.

God understands each of us. He has intentionally designed us with varied strengths and weakness so we would be mutually dependent upon one another and truly function as one body.

Most of the studies I have done have divided personality traits into four major classifications. The terms I use most often for identification purposes are Greek terms: *sanguine, choleric, melancholy* and *phlegmatic*. The Holy Spirit has given me insight and discernment in this area. He has helped me discern the potential and witness the development of many people as they yielded their personalities to the ministry of the Holy Spirit and allowed Him to bring them to wholeness.

Personality Types Defined

You may be categorized as a *sanguine* personality—known for your high-energy, fun-loving, outgoing temperament. Whatever you do, you do to the extreme, whether it is studying, praying, cleaning house or talking.

A leadership role challenges you to learn organizational skills, take control of your tongue and pray for discernment. Quiet times in a prayer group may be uncomfortable. This is a chance for you to be still before God. You will be tempted just to "go with the flow," but too often situations spin out of control without a certain amount of structure.

Submit to the control of the Holy Spirit, who is working with you to develop the fruit of self-control. Your optimistic, sunny disposition draws people. Continue to develop God-given leadership skills.

Love for God and His people should compel all of us who are leaders to learn self-discipline and walk in the Spirit so we can become better servants. This is the true heart of a leader.

> **Let this mind be in you, which was also in Christ Jesus: who, being in the form of God, thought it not robbery to be equal with God: but made himself of no reputation, and took upon him the form of a servant, and was made in the likeness of men.**
> **Philippians 2:5-7**

Sanguine leaders enjoy loud, boisterous times of prayer. Still, they expect the quiet times and allow others the opportunity to express themselves.

A *choleric* personality is outgoing and independent. He is task-oriented and a natural-born leader. He lives to achieve and organizes quickly. As a prayer leader, he may place a demand on prayer partners to move from one prayer subject to another rapidly. His tendency is to attempt to manage people rather than things.

The choleric leader comes with his list of things to do and is happiest when every prayer subject has been covered, fulfilling the need for achievement. Often the prayers of this group are short and to the point and move like popcorn. This type of leader is challenged to displace a bossy attitude with humility and meekness. He has to learn that God—not performance—is his sufficiency.

The anointing makes the choleric personality an effective spiritual leader. As he yields to the anointing and develops the fruit of the Spirit, short-tempered behavior gives way to patience. He learns to make room for the leadership of the Holy Spirit and to allow the expression of the other personalities in the group. His tendency to be self-willed and overbearing is overcome by the love of God as He grows in grace and in the knowledge of Jesus Christ.

The *melancholy* leader has a well-organized plan to get things done perfectly. This personality type is quieter, deeper and more thoughtful. He starts his prayer group at its appointed time, even if he is the only one present, and he ends on time. Deviation from his plan may cause a personal crisis until he learns to trust the Holy Spirit's guidance.

The strengths of the melancholy leader include sensitivity to the needs of others. He is prayerful and serious, orderly and intellectually astute. Through intimacy with God, he seeks to understand himself, pull down a stronghold of suspicion and overcome a critical attitude. He no longer demands perfection of everyone else, looking instead for opportunities to serve others. Walking in the Spirit, he goes forward, his conduct controlled by the Holy Spirit.

When caught in uncomfortable situations, his insulated walls may go up for self-preservation. More than any other personality, the melancholy leader wants to achieve perfection and has an intense desire to serve God. A prayer group with a melancholy leader is very methodical and usually quiet and reflective.

The *phlegmatic* personality accepts a leadership role by repeated invitation only. His fear of criticism often prevents him from developing God-given leadership abilities. His major strength is service. He is a comfort and support to others, often bringing peace out of chaos.

Through intimacy with God, he is able to overcome an attitude of indifference and provide balance when situations get out of kilter. Sometimes his prayer group loses its focus of praying for others as he ministers to a hurting individual—his preferred activity. He doesn't throw out challenges and will even skirt the truth to avoid confrontation and keep the peace.

Lead by Serving

When we accept the God-given authority to lead a group, that responsibility places a demand on us to serve rather than to "lord it over others." The Bible says that where the Spirit of the Lord is, there is liberty. (2 Cor. 3:17.) This sense of freedom gives prayer team members the liberty to learn how to be led by the Holy Spirit in prayer while following the accepted guidelines.

When praying for or under the authority of a church or ministry, prayer leaders need to know the God-given vision of that church or ministry. Our prayers prepare the way for the vision to be fulfilled.

Ask God for His provision. Seek God to know how to pray more effectively. Don't turn coward. Don't give up or quit. Persevere in prayer.

Carefully avoid violating another person's God-given authority as head of a ministry. Recognize lines of authority, and fulfill the role as a minister of helps. Pray to move obstacles that would prevent the leader from hearing and following God's directives for the ministry.

Intercessors must resist the human, soulish urge to "fix" the leader and refuse to assume responsibilities that do not belong to them. As they pray within scriptural guidelines, the scope of influence—for both the intercessors and the pastor—will enlarge within the limits of their commissions.

God has charged us to pray for those who will give an account to Him for all ministry decisions. Therefore, as members of intercessory prayer groups, we are to *stand with* our leader in orderly array, enforcing the triumphant victory of Jesus our Lord.

Pastors and ministry leaders are often inundated with suggestions—many of which simply arise out of criticism. Ministry leaders are open game for opinions and ideas from those who believe they have a better understanding of God's plan for the local assembly.

Don't allow yourself to fall into that trap. Instead, pray scripturally for your spiritual leaders, whose work it is to watch over the souls of God's people. **Give them reason to report joyfully about you to the Lord and not with sorrow, for then you will suffer for it too** (Heb.13:17 TLB). Be a cohesive member of the ministry. Never bring about division.

When you establish a prayer group, it is important to know the prayer focus of the group. I suggest that you maintain notebooks with the minutes of past meetings. Then refer to these notebooks when you sense that you are wandering away from your assignment.

Do not overextend the direction and purpose of your group. Groups who attempt to incorporate every aspect of prayer in a designated time period usually find themselves leaving tired and frustrated because they do not feel that the prayer assignment has been fulfilled.

Determine the God-given assignments of your prayer group. Fulfilling God's agenda will edify you, strengthen you and build you up. Furthermore, God will be glorified!

Clear Communication Promotes Unity

How can two walk together except they agree? *Communication* is of paramount importance when believers work together, requiring the determination of everyone involved to listen to another's point of view. In the end, however, the final decision rests with the leader.

As the leader of a ministry, I look for people who will listen and give me feedback. God has blessed me with a prayer coordinator who expresses her ideas and thoughts. At times, we agree to seek God for greater understanding on a given subject and then to schedule another meeting.

Whereas I welcome change and tend to act impulsively, my prayer coordinator is uncomfortable with change and moves slowly. This "check-and-balance system" is very important and helpful to me. Together we make up a good prayer team. We are not afraid to submit to one another. There are times that we go with the plan God has revealed to her. However, she has never failed to cooperate with my final decision.

We have learned that through prayer, good communication and then more prayer, God will surpass our discomfort with a viewpoint different from our own. We see these times as growth opportunities. Reasoning together demands that we seek out the wisdom that is from above as defined in James 3:17. The *Phillips* translation reads:

Wisdom that comes from above is first pure, then peace-loving, gentle, approachable, full of merciful thoughts and kindly actions, straightforward, with no hint of hypocrisy. And the peacemakers go on quietly sowing for a harvest of righteousness.

If God has called you to pray for a ministry, get into agreement with the vision of that ministry. Give your full support to its leader with love, prayer and faith.

Guidelines for Group Leaders

When God appoints individuals to a prayer group, they are His agents of prayer, and He will reward them by allowing them to develop and grow in His grace. One of His instruments for this process is the prayer group leader whom He calls and equips for service.

God doesn't limit His call for leadership to certain personality types. He calls people regardless of their personalities, knowing His strength is made perfect in weakness. (2 Cor. 12:9.)

A God-called leader is one who has learned to recognize and obey spiritual authority. The authority to carry out this role as prayer leader is delegated by the ministry leader.

To serve others in a leadership role, a leader has to keep a vigil over attitudes and motives, while maintaining an intimate relationship with God. This requires a commitment to God, to the leadership and the body of Christ. It is an act of love.

If you are appointed as a prayer group leader, your goal is to stay on course while promoting harmony within the group. Prayerfully plan and organize each meeting under the direction of the Holy Spirit. Know the vision of the ministry. Understand clearly its mission and communicate those guidelines and goals clearly to group members. Prepare pledge cards, and ask each member to sign an appropriate statement of commitment.

United prayer is a powerful form of prayer. As the group leader, you must determine the prayer focus, giving simple directions and acknowledging the presence of the Holy Spirit.

Should you become aware that a person in the group is having difficulty praying in a particular area, you may take a few minutes for open discussion, answering any questions pertaining to the proposed prayer project.

But don't get sidetracked trying to "fix" anyone, and don't get pulled off into a teaching mode. Keep in mind the purpose for which the group has come together. If necessary, rather than take up everyone's time, schedule an appointment with the person needing more clarification or attention. However, it is sometimes wise to delay a prayer assignment and deal with personal apprehensions and misunderstandings within the group.

At times, a prayer assignment will expose a need in an individual who is praying. Be available to meet privately with this person. Plan another, more appropriate time to pray for one another, that all may be healed and restored to a spiritual tone of mind and heart.

Avoid taking on the cares of individual members and becoming emotionally entangled with them. However, take the time to do follow-up and develop good communication skills. Promote the harmony that is so vital for you to come together and make a symphony in prayer before the throne of grace. Depend on the Holy Spirit to give you words of comfort and encouragement for members in need.

When you do not have a ready answer, do not be afraid to say, "I don't know. Let's pray and get back together later." Then search out resources, go to your superior for answers and pray, pray, pray.

Practical Duties of a Group Leader

The prayer group leader is responsible for:

1. Praying for those who are uniting with him in prayer.

2. Scheduling regular meetings with his ministry leader.

3. Organizing prayer groups.

4. Training others in prayer leadership

5. Teaching and instructing groups as needed.

6. Uniting the people in the group by presenting specific prayer projects.

7. Maintaining a log of prayer assignments and any Scriptures relating to prayer requests. (This responsibility may be delegated to someone in the group.)

8. Scheduling times for fellowship and personal ministry with the group.

Often members of a prayer group do not know each other personally. But Paul admonished believers—with good reason—to seek to know one another after the Spirit rather than after the flesh.

As your prayer group meets week after week, personality traits become more evident. Understanding your personality enables you to make room for other personality types. So attend workshops on prayer, leadership and organization. Learn to respond rather than react, and sharpen your communication skills in order to work with and lead people.

God calls you not because of *your* merit but to further His own purpose. Know yourself! Ask God to reveal your personal strengths and weaknesses. Learn to be objective, and avoid making an issue out of personal differences.

Leaders: Stay Sensitive
to Needs in the Group

Leaders who set boundaries and define responsibilities give their prayer groups the direction needed to stay focused.

Guidelines are flexible and are not intended to put you in a box. Avoid rigidity because some situations will arise that require emergency prayer.

The spiritually astute leader usually recognizes when an individual is overtaken with an adverse situation that requires immediate attention. Sometimes a fellow-laborer is so burdened with the cares of this world that he cannot enter into prayer for others. He may not even be able to pray for himself!

This is a time to bear one another person's burdens. A few minutes of quiet time, playing a music tape or gently laying hands on the individual will release him to unite with the group for the prayer assignments. Let love govern how you lead in every situation.

As your group becomes closely knit together, allow the Holy Spirit to lead you to an individual in your group who will be there for you as a support person. Call one another outside the appointed prayer group time.

Be willing to reach out; you need one another for support, wise counsel, encouragement and agreement.

One of the greatest hindrances to developing healthy relationships in the group is a form of hypersensitivity: in other words, a person's belief that every statement is directed toward him or her personally. But if a person knows that God has planted him in a particular group, he should stay with it and allow the cooperate anointing to bring healing to wounds caused by past experiences of rejection.

The leader establishes the guidelines for personal ministry. Valuable time can be wasted in tying to "fix" hurting individuals. You are not called to do the work of the Holy Spirit. He is a competent Convictor and Convincer. He is the Master Builder and "Fixer-Upper."

As colaborers together with God and one another, we are to empathize, validate, affirm, comfort, edify and pray each for the other. In the safety of this group environment, we trust each other enough to confess our faults (slips, false steps, offenses and sins) at those appropriate times and to pray for one another.

Do not attempt to remove the splinter in another's eye while continuing to allow the plank in your own eye to remain. No one can remove that "plank" for you except God, who is effectually at work in you. (1 Thess. 2:13.)

Each member brings something to the table—both positive and negative, both strengths and weaknesses. Do not be afraid of change. When others offer opinions that differ from yours, take time to evaluate before you reject their ideas. God may be exposing a need for a change of attitude or revealing wisdom for which you have asked.

Remember, change produces change. When you submit to the ministry of transformation by the Holy Spirit, your change in attitude and behavior will influence others to change. You determine your influence, your integrity and your identification. Be an example of righteousness, and say with the apostle Paul, "Follow me as I follow Christ." (1 Cor. 11:1.)

Guidelines for Group Members

If you are a group member rather than a leader, you also have important responsibilities to fulfill. When you join a prayer group, you are making a commitment that requires accountability to other members, as well as to the group leader and to the pastor. You should welcome that accountability and recognize the lines of authority in the group.

Small groups provide an opportunity for you to receive emotional healing as you grow spiritually in the grace and knowledge of Jesus Christ. However, while praying with the group, you must determine not to focus on your own needs but to maintain the prayer focus as presented by your prayer leader.

As a group member, you must be teachable, willing to yield to reason and respectful of the assigned leader. You must also be a student of God's Word and a worshiper of the true God.

When you have difficulty with a prayer assignment, be straightforward in expressing your concerns. However, keep in mind James' instruction to be slow to speak and quick to listen. (James 1:19.) Approach any differences with a desire to understand rather than a demand to be understood.

Your leader has to make decisions based on information that he may not be at liberty to divulge. Exercise patience, and ask for wisdom until all is made clear. The final decision within the group resides with the leader.

Cooperate with your leader, and God will reward your faithfulness. Be faithful to pursue your personal prayer assignments—praying for your family, your government and any other prayer opportunities. Your faithfulness to God and another man's ministry will be rewarded. God is mindful of your labors!

As a group member, your responsibilities are to:

1. Set aside your personal desires and needs in favor of others who cannot or do not know how to pray for themselves.

2. Be unwavering in your commitment to God, your pastor or ministry leader, your group leader and to the particular ministry for which you are praying.

3. Prepare your heart ahead of time. Judge yourself according to the Word of God. Should you have any wrong attitudes (resentment, unforgiveness or criticism), submit them to the Holy Spirit. Using the keys to the kingdom, bind your mind, your will and your emotions to the will, plan and purposes of God for the day. Loose your soul from wrong attitudes, wrong thought patterns and wrong ideas. (I recommend reading *Shattering Your Strongholds* by Liberty Savard.)

4. Cooperate with the leader, and follow the flow of the corporate anointing.

5. Share that which you believe you have received from the Holy Spirit at the appropriate time. Keeping prayer notes will help you stay with the group. Make notes and share them at an appropriate time.

6. Be prepared to work in other areas of ministry. Praying empowers you for the task.

7. Spend time alone with God, drawing from His strength and preparing your heart to receive and pray the intercession of Jesus.

8. As a team member, make allowances for others. Never monopolize the allotted time. Trust God to meet your needs and your family's needs.

Diversities of Groups

Over the years, I have attended many prayer groups. In doing so, I have discovered that each has its own personality and unique functions. That's why it is important to make room for one another.

For example, some groups storm their way into prayer with an almost incredible viciousness, releasing a powerful energy field. They go through the gyrations of a wrestling match with unseen forces—screaming, yelling and throwing their arms about wildly. They launch themselves spiritually, physically and emotionally into the fight against their unseen opponents.

Other groups may pray according to a set pattern, joining their voices together in united prayer. They follow written scriptural prayers, lifting their hearts as one before the Father. Another group may sit in a circle, praying one-sentence prayers.

In still another group, everyone may first share their prayer requests and then kneel, praying in an atmosphere of reverence. In this group, you may hear quiet sobbing, low, rumbling voices, praise, Scripture prayers and praying in the Spirit. Quietly the members lift their hearts and voices simultaneously, praying individually. This is commonly known as a concert prayer, with each member giving voice to the burden of his or her heart.

A common practice in prayer groups is to announce the topics for prayer with applicable Scriptures as a point of reference. The members pray in accordance with the leader at the direction of the Holy Spirit—lifting up each prayer subject one by one. Others write all prayer requests on a board. Then as people file in to the meeting, they select subjects for which they are led to pray.

Some groups pray loudly; others pray quietly, even silently. Some use praise as their primary weapon of warfare, stating their needs to the Father in the form of thanksgiving and praise. Other groups begin to moan and groan, believing that the Holy Spirit will give them utterance for travail of the Spirit.

Walk in Discernment

As we draw nearer to the coming of the Lord, we can expect to see more phenomenal supernatural signs. Discernment is essential.

For instance, when a prayer group places great emphasis on physical activity, the members may end up with a form of supernatural demonstrations that are void of power. Therefore, stay alert; when you see warning signs, stop and seek God. Ask yourself, *Is this a wrong spirit at work or a violation of the Scriptures? Or am I reacting to something that is uncomfortable to my flesh?*

Always approach any situation expecting to learn something. It may be that you learn what not to do, or you may receive greater insight and enter into another level of prayer.

Take the time to rely on the Holy Spirit's leadership. You can't contain God in a box and dictate every moment of every prayer session. He may ask you to take a certain action that releases a true demonstration of His power. Obedience is better than sacrifice.

I thank God both for those with whom I have disagreed and for those with whom I have agreed. I have learned from both.

Be Open to New Members

You will become bonded with others in your group. However, remember intercessory prayer groups are not for the purpose of forming cliques.

Exclusive groups that are usually not open to outsiders suggest they are on a higher plane of prayer. They sometimes say that if a person is not in the Spirit, he cannot understand certain practices. This makes prayer seem mystical and eerie.

If God wants your group to be a training ground for others, make room for new group members. This is a good opportunity to review and restate the purpose of the group. Make sure the new member is welcomed, even though it may be uncomfortable for you in the beginning.

Once again, keep in mind that change will produce change, often bringing us to another level of growth. If God has sent the new member, cooperate with His plan. It will benefit both you and the newcomer.

God's Word does not return to Him void of power and purpose. When God's people come together with one mind and one purpose, intercessory efforts will produce prayers that glorify God and avail much.

Fulfilling Our God-Assigned Position

Every prayer group has its own "personality" based on a number of variables, such as:

- The purpose of the group (which includes the God-given prayer assignment and the way the Holy Spirit chooses to approach that assignment in prayer).

- The personalities and temperaments of group members.

- The unique giftings and callings resident within the group.

All of these elements combine to distinguish the "flow" and "flavor" of each prayer group. Therefore, there is no singular "right way" to conduct a prayer group. The one common rule that all prayer groups must follow to be effective is to do all in love and in obedience to the Word and the Spirit of God.

The number-one challenge with prayer groups arises when individual groups believe that the manner in which they conduct their prayer service is the one and only "correct" manner and that everyone else is wrong. This stronghold of rigidity becomes a tool of the enemy to inject intimidation, distrust and disharmony into the church. His intention is to stop real, heart-felt, fervent prayer on behalf of the saints.

Satan is particularly aggressive in his attempt to stop evangelistic intercession. But greater is He who is in us than he that would divide and conquer! (1 John 4:4.)

God is a many-faceted God. He works with each of us according to the measure of grace He has given us. Each person and each prayer group is unique, and God includes us all in His great and glorious plan.

Our symphony of prayer will exalt the One who has called us and encourage those who labor to fulfill the plan of God in these final hours before the culmination of all things. Together, united in purpose and spirit, we can raise an impenetrable fortress of fervent prayer, offsetting the onslaught of the wicked one and erecting a mighty wall around Zion.

The walls around the body of Christ are made up of people who submit to God and resist the devil. God has always maintained an unseen prayer network comprised of lively stones positioned in the wall as He wills.

As watchers on that wall, we are to stand in the gap, praying for those who are wounded by the enemy and for others who cover their sins with religious rituals.

Today God is raising up a network of prayer ministries. If we bind ourselves to obedience and determine to follow after His Spirit, we will stand shoulder to shoulder in orderly array. Then each one of us will fulfill our God-assigned position, as together our lives create the wall surrounding the spiritual Jerusalem.

Commitment To Pray

Father, in the name of Jesus, I offer up thanksgiving that You have called me to be a fellow workman—a joint promoter and a laborer together—with and for You. I commit myself to pray and not to turn coward—faint, lose heart, or give up.

Fearlessly and confidently and boldly I draw near to the throne of grace that I may receive mercy and find grace to help in good time for every need—appropriate help and well-timed help, coming just when I (and others) need it. This is the confidence that I have in You, that if I ask anything according to Your will, You hear me: and if I know that You hear me, whatsoever I ask, I know that I have the petitions that I desired of You.

When I do not know what prayer to offer and how to offer it worthily as I ought, I thank You, Father, that the Holy Spirit comes to my aid and bears me up in my weakness (my inability to produce results). He, the Holy Spirit, goes to meet my supplication and pleads in my behalf with unspeakable yearnings and groanings too deep for utterance. And He Who searches the hearts of men knows what is in the mind of the Holy Spirit. The Holy Spirit intercedes and pleads in behalf of the saints according to and in harmony with God's will. Therefore, I am assured and know that (God being a partner in my labor) all things work together and are (fitting into a plan) for my good, because I love God and am called according to (His) design and purpose.

I do not fret or have any anxiety about anything, but in every circumstance and in everything by prayer and petition (definite requests) with thanksgiving continue to make my wants (and the wants of others) known to God. Whatever I ask for in prayer, I believe that it is granted to me, and I will receive it.

The earnest (heartfelt, continued) prayer of a righteous man makes tremendous power available—dynamic in its working. Father, I live in You—abide vitally united to You—and Your words remain in me and continue to live in my heart. Therefore, I ask whatever I will, and it shall be done for me. When I bear (produce) much fruit (through prayer), You, Father, are honored and glorified. Hallelujah! Amen.

Scripture References

1 Corinthians 3:8 AMP	*Philippians 4:6* AMP
Luke 18:1 AMP	*Mark 11:24* AMP
Hebrews 4:16 AMP	*James 5:16b* AMP
1 John 5:14,15	*John 15:7,8* AMP
Romans 8:26-29 AMP	

Endnotes

Chapter 2
[1] Vine, s.v. "grace," Vol. 2, pp. 169-171.

Chapter 3
[1] Bounds, p. 40.
[2] Ibid.

Chapter 4
[1] Vine, s.v. "travail," Vol. 4 pp. 150,151.
[2] Strong, "Greek," entry #5605, p. 79.

Chapter 5
[1] Copeland, "Improving Communication." *Prayers That Avail Much, Volume 1*, p. 177.
[2] Hayford, p. 5.

Chapter 6
[1] Murray, p. 32.
[2] Copeland, *Prayers That Avail Much, Volume 1*, p. 72.
[3] Copeland, *Prayers That Avail Much, Volume 2*, p. 106.

Chapter 7
[1] Penn-Lewis, p. 19.
[2] Carter, pp. 97,98.

Chapter 8
[1] Copeland, "Adoration: 'Hallowed Be Thy Name'" *Prayers That Avail Much, Vol. 2*, p. 49.
[2] Unger, p. 1086.
[3] Pollard, Adelaide and George C. Stebbins. "Have Thine Own Way, Lord."

Chapter 9
[1] Strong, "Greek," entry #3671, p.52.

Chapter 10
[1] Rivera, p. 7.
[2] Vine, s.v. "wrestle," Vol. 4, p. 239.
[3] *Webster's New World College Dictionary, Third Edition*, p. 1351.
[4] Ibid.
[5] Ibid.
[6] Ibid, p. 1486.
[7] Ibid.
[8] Ibid.

[9] Wuest, p. 141.

[10] Wuest, p. 142.

Chapter 11

[1] *Webster's New World Dictionary of American English, Third Edition of American English,* p. 599.

References

Bounds, E.M. *The Possibility of Prayer*. Springdale: Whitaker House, 1994.

Carter, Howard. *Questions and Answers on Spiritual Gifts*. Tulsa: Harrison House, 1976.

Copeland, Germaine. "Husbands." *Prayers That Avail Much, Volume 1*. Tulsa: Harrison House, 1999.

Copeland, Germaine. "Improving Communication." *Prayers That Avail Much, Volume 1*. Tulsa: Harrison House, 1999.

Copeland, Germaine. "The New Creation Marriage." *Prayers That Avail Much, Volume 2*. Tulsa: Harrison House, 1999.

Hayford, Jack. *Prayer Is Invading the Impossible*. New York: Ballantine Books, 1983.

Murray, Andrew. *The Prayer Life*. Springdale: Whitaker House, 1981.

Penn-Lewis, Jessie. *The Spiritual Warfare*. Northants, Great Britain: Stanley L. Hunt Printers, Ltd.,

Rivera, Dr. Mario E. *Facing Unresolved Conflicts*. Los Angeles: New Leaf Press, Inc., 1992.

Strong, James. *Strong's Exhaustive Concordance of the Bible*. "Hebrew and Chaldee Dictionary." "Greek Dictionary of the New Testament." Nashville: Abingdon, 1890.

Unger, Merrill F. et al. *Unger's Bible Dictionary, Third Edition*. Chicago: The Moody Bible Institute of Chicago. 1966.

Vine, W.E. *Expository Dictionary of New Testament Words*. Old Tappan: Fleming H. Revell, 1940.

Webster's New World Dictionary of American English, Third Edition. New York: Webster's New World, 1994.

Wuest, Kenneth S. *Word Studies in the Greek New Testament, Vol. 1*. Grand Rapids: William B. Eerdmans' Publishing Company, 1978.

About the Author

Germaine Griffin Copeland, founder and president of Word Ministries, Inc., is the author of the *Prayers That Avail Much Family Books.* Her writings provide scriptural prayer instruction to help you pray effectively for those things that concern you and your family and for other prayer assignments. Her teachings on prayer, the personal growth of the intercessor, emotional healing and related subjects have brought understanding, hope, healing and liberty to the discouraged and emotionally wounded. She is a woman of prayer and praise whose highest form of worship is the study of God's Word. Her greatest desire is to know God.

Word Ministries, Inc. is a prayer and teaching ministry. Germaine believes that God has called her to teach the practical application of the Word of Truth for a practical prayer life and victorious living. After years of searching diligently for truth and trying again and again to come out of depression, she decided that she was a mistake. Out of the depths of despair she called upon the name of the Lord, and the light of God's presence permeated the room where she was sitting.

It was in that moment that she experienced the warmth of God's love; old things passed away, and she became brand new. She discovered a motivation for living—life had purpose. Living in the presence of God, she has found unconditional love and acceptance, healing for crippled emotions, contentment that overcomes depression, peace in the midst of adverse circumstances and grace for developing healthy relationships. The ongoing process of transformation evolved into praying for others.

Germaine is the daughter of Reverend A. H. "Buck" Griffin and the late Donnis Brock Griffin. She and her husband, Everette, have four children, and their prayer challenges increase as more grandchildren and great-grandchildren are born. Germaine and Everette reside in Sandy Springs, a suburb of Atlanta, Georgia.

Word Ministries' offices are located in Historic Roswell, 38 Sloan Street, Roswell, Georgia 30075.

You may contact Germaine Copeland by writing:

Germaine Copeland
Word Ministries, Inc.
38 Sloan Street
Roswell, Georgia 30075
or calling 770-518-1065

*Please include your prayer requests
and comments when you write.*

Other Books by Germaine Copeland

A Call to Prayer

Prayers That Avail Much—Volume 1
A portable gift book

Prayers That Avail Much—Volume 2
A portable gift book

Prayers That Avail Much—Volume 3
A portable gift book

Oraciones Con Poder
Prayers That Avail Much
Spanish Edition

Prayers That Avail Much for Business Professionals

Prayers That Avail Much Leather—Special Edition

Prayers That Avail Much for Mothers
Pocket Size

Prayers That Avail Much for Mothers
Leather

Prayers That Avail Much for Fathers

Prayers That Avail Much for Teens
Revised pocket edition

Prayers That Avail Much Daily Calendar

**Additional copies of this book are
available from your local bookstore.**

Harrison House
Tulsa, Oklahoma

In Canada books are available from:
Word Alive, P.O. Box 670
Niverville, Manitoba CANADA ROA 1E0

The Harrison House Vision

Proclaiming the truth and the power

Of the Gospel of Jesus Christ

With excellence

Challenging Christians to

Live victoriously,

Grow spiritually,

Know God intimately.